How Republicans Became the Party of Stupid

Introducing: The Tea Party

Justin Kase

To my mom Joanne , whose been a symbol of resilience and strength and gone beyond the call of duty to be there for me throughout my entire life. Words cannot express my gratitude to you.

In memory of my brother Shawn...I really miss you a whole lot.

In memory of our sweet angel Summer...you're not gone and you'll never be forgotten.

Special shout out to the fellas: Vince, Nelson, Norvel, Moo and Bryant who had to put up with me and constantly listen to different sections of this book. I truly appreciate your patience and now I can annoy you guys with other things. Thanks for the ear fellas.

To my baby Sunday: One day after laughing at my work and probably shaking your head at how ridiculous I can be at times, you'll still realize how much I love you.

Special thanks to my wife Jessica. Without you this book would not be possible. It must be known that I am truly grateful for you and for the fact that you put up with me on an everyday basis. I'm glad to know that you understand that you are forced to do this for the rest of your life, because there's no way you can get rid of me. I love you. To say that your devotion and your loyalty is unique is an understatement. Your love and support is unmatched.

PROLOGUE

Mass flooding on the upper East Coast led to billions of dollars in damages. Tornados ripped through Alabama and other parts of the country causing catastrophic disasters as well. Nature was wreaking havoc everywhere in 2011. Ordinary people saw their lives turned upside down in the blink of an eye. Others lost their lives. FEMA seemed to be prepared. Even outgoing Republican Governor Chris Christie of New Jersey praised the Obama Administration for "a fine job".

FEMA's funding was understandably beginning to dry up. It was obvious that a lot of work was still to be done in the states that suffered the most damage. Congress in a normal world simply produces language in their annual spending bill to replenish FEMA. The money it costs to fund FEMA is less than one percent of the entire federal budget, so it's never a problem. Especially in 2011, where so many people across the country were in dire need of FEMA's assistance. With these circumstances, only a callous, cold-hearted, shit- for- brains bastard would do something stupid and malicious like block the funding for FEMA. Without further ado, that person is none other than Eric Cantor. Eric is the House Majority Leader. He is a Republican from Virginia who happens to be such a staunch fiscal conservative that he wanted to refuse FEMA the needed funds unless cuts were made to other government programs. Preferably programs he doesn't like. This, of course, was not political grandstanding on the backs of victims who just saw their lives destroyed. This was a man who refused to go against his core principles.

That's right folks…*everything* has to be paid for. No matter how big or how small, every crisis and every situation known to mankind must be paid for. He does not believe in adding one penny to the deficit. Good for him. I am glad he's not the kind of guy who would vote for unpaid tax cuts for the rich, or two unpaid wars, or a prescription drug plan that would help blow gigantic holes in the deficit. Oh wait a minute…he did vote for all those things that were not paid for.

Well, I guess you have to start somewhere, so let's deny flood victims in need of assistance. Even though it's a gazillion times cheaper than that damn prescription drug program.

In April 2011, the so-called "titanic budget battle" took place. Republicans threatened to shut down the government because of five million dollars that would be used to fund Planned Parenthood. After agreeing on how to spend the first trillion, Republicans could not tolerate that extra five million going towards Planned Parenthood. This was about as petty as the owner of the Los Angeles Lakers telling Kobe Bryant, "Son, I am willing to give you a $999,999 bonus, but as for that extra <u>one</u> dollar you're asking for, it's becoming a real sticking point."

To the dismay of Republicans, a mass majority of Americans failed to understand such a bold stance against an organization that helps about 5 million low-income women receive needed healthcare. After realizing they were going to be blamed for the government shutdown, Republicans struck a deal with the White House. The deal would produce a whopping 380 billion dollars in spending cuts…oops, I mean 38 billion in spending cuts, and that was actually just an accounting gimmick. The Congressional Budget Office reported or "exposed" that only 352 *million* was cut. The good news is that Planned Parenthood survived the unprovoked witch hunt.

Then the real fun came. In June there was an actual threat not to raise the debt ceiling. Everyone from all over the political and economic spectrum agreed that 4 trillion dollars should be cut over the next ten years. Democrats were willing to give Republicans every spending cut known to man. Cut Medicare, cut Social Security, cut their hair, cut their throats, etc…

In exchange for all this, Democrats wanted taxes raised on the rich so they could feel that they were not completely bullied and bitch slapped again.

The deal President Obama offered Republicans behind closed doors was so sweet that John Boehner, the House Speaker, reportedly swallowed the cigarette he was smoking while chanting, "Yes We Can!" on the White House lawn. Okay, I made that part up, but he was pretty excited. In fact, he was so excited that he ran back to his fellow House Republicans to share the news of their victory. He told Republicans that he'd just suckered the president into the deal of a lifetime. The biggest deficit reduction package in the history of planet Earth.

It was a Republican dream come true. Cut entitlements, massive cuts to discretionary spending, spending freezes, you name it. In exchange for all these spending cuts the president wanted tax hikes on the rich.

Eric Cantor swiftly stepped in. He told the House Speaker to go back to the president and tell him "no deal". Nice try, Mr. Slick President. The president wants to give Republicans 90 percent of what they want to save the country from its first ever default. Well, it won't work.

It's all or nothing. So what happened? Neither side gets anything and the nation's fiscal problems remained unsolved. The country goes from angry to downright disgusted.

At the end of 2011, another really stupid skirmish breaks out between the jackasses known as elected officials. The White House decided it wanted to extend the payroll tax cut for another year. This middle class tax cut has been pretty popular with the public. Republicans decided that they would only vote for an extension if the tax cuts were paid for.

Amazingly, when the tax cut was passed a year earlier it was not paid for. In fact, 858 billion dollars was added to the deficit because of the package that was agreed to between the president and congressional Republicans. Besides the middle class payroll tax cut in the package, there was the Bush tax cuts for the rich along with tax cuts for such vital needs as NASCAR. Now how's that for a stimulus package?

Republicans have always claimed tax cuts pay for themselves. In fact, this article of faith is one reason why they always blow holes in the deficit whenever they're in charge of the White House. Of course those huge tax cuts also featured huge tax breaks for the rich. This package did not. It was strictly for the middle class.

Once again, it was good to see Republicans stand up for their core convictions. Front and center, as usual, was Eric Cantor. He is the man who wants everything paid for—all of a sudden. The Party of Tax Cuts was about to allow everybody's taxes to go up if the package was not paid for. This was a complete reversal of their ideology.

The president wanted to pay for the tax cuts by raising taxes on millionaires. This was like trying to convince David Duke to escort Al Sharpton to a dinner party in honor of Dr. Martin Luther King Jr. Not going to happen.

So, Republicans finally decided that paying for the tax cuts is not all that important after all. Instead, they agree to pass the extension on one condition. The president was to say yay or nay on the Keystone XL Pipeline Project. This is a pipeline that if built would run from Canada to Texas. After a two month fight and public pressure to quit acting like they all bought some good dope from Paris Hilton, Republicans passed the two month extension. These are the same Republicans that passed a massive tax cut package twice when George W. Bush was president, and passed another one in 2010. None of these packages were paid for. Did I mention that the unpaid packages were way more expensive?

Now, I am not trying to imply that Republicans are not as enthusiastic to pass the tax cut because it's only for 160 million middle class taxpayers. The fact that this tax cut for the middle class is "suddenly" a drag on the deficit might be irrelevant. It just looks a little suspicious that

Republicans do somersaults to protect tax cuts for the rich, but turn a routine extension of a middle class tax cut into a freak show. Just a bit strange, that's all.

These are some of the highlights from the Republican Party of 2011. A party that seems to have lost its mind.

It's common for both parties to play the role of obstructionist when they are not in power. Democrats played games with Bush, but this is a bit different. This has a different intensity and determination. It's as if it's no longer about Democrat vs. Republican. It's turned into me against you. Republicans have taken the game to a whole new level, a very dangerous one at that. The debt ceiling fiasco might not just be a close call. It could be a glimpse of things to come. This is because Republicans have moved so far to the right that they are inching closer and closer to the nuthouse.

I may sound like a biased liberal, but I love to chastise Democrats as well when the facts show just cause for such occasions. The thing is I don't need to. The voters just did that in 2010. Since then the Democrats have been on their best behavior. 2010 sobered Democrats to the point that they almost make me want to throw up.

When Republicans asked voters to put them back in charge of the House, they claimed they were sober and ready to lead again. They are leading alright. Leading everyone into a state of depression and disgust. But both parties have issues and both have idiots inside their parties, but while Democrats have grown more timid, Republicans have grown more detached from reality.

This is all pretty common knowledge. The media is scared to death of being labeled liberal so they constantly sugarcoat the facts and walk on eggshells. After all, you might be talked about on (gulp) Fox News!!! That's like some kind of media damnation or first class ticket to forced retirement. We must all watch what we say because Fox News might verbally whip us into submission. Well, screw Fox News. How's that?! Any morons who have the macho-looking bimbo Ann Coulter on their network three times a week is hard for me to take seriously.

In fact, Fox News is not conservative-leaning like other humble media outlets gently put it. Nope, Fox News is downright full of shit. Let's just call a spade a spade. While Republicans turn Washington into a House of Horrors, Fox News does everything possible to spin the story and justify the conservative nut jobs in Congress.

Many claim to love this country but act as if they are scared to death to be bluntly honest. While some networks like Fox are not scared to be bluntly *dis*honest. It's okay to be a Democrat and criticize your own party. Just like it's okay to be a Republican and admit when the president does something right. It is an act of treason, however, to put party above country. It is a cowardly display of partisanship to hope the unemployment rate stays high so that the president might lose in November.

Many in this country have grown so concerned about who wins the election that it's easy to become desensitized to the suffering of others. Every piece of data and evidence becomes justification for the cheerleading of a particular party. It's so easy to overlook the fact that the numbers represent real people. Their suffering becomes secondary to the team.

In the meantime, Democrats are still so shell-shocked from the brutal ass whipping they received in 2010 that they are starving for compromise. This is a good thing. The problem is the Republicans. They have no political incentive to compromise. Their base says all or nothing. This strategy has hurt the country in a number of ways but it's been great for politics. Why stop now? This is the same base that worships Ronald Reagan, yet Reagan compromised on everything. He showed compromise can take you a long way, and get a lot done.

So what happened? How did the Party of the Gipper go into Coo-Cooville? How did "Morning in America" turn into nighttime in the nuthouse? Better yet, why did right wingers tie themselves into knots just to become right wing extremist who no longer make sense? To understand the present condition of today's Republicans we should take a glimpse back.

1 | THE BUSH ERA AND COMPASSIONATE CONSERVATISM

To truly understand the Bush era, we should take a quick glimpse at the Clinton era.

For several years Bill Clinton out maneuvered Republicans at every turn. He absorbed every scandal and embarrassment that came his way. Through it all he managed to come out smelling like a rose. I mean, so what if he disgraced the highest office in the land on numerous occasions! The guy plays a saxophone and he has a problem with stuffing cheeseburgers down his face. What's not to love?

The country also prospered immensely during the Clinton era. Under Clinton, over 20 million jobs were created and the budget was balanced for four straight years. A liberal Clinton showed he could govern from the center and move the country forward. When Clinton left office, the unemployment rate was low and his budget was projected to produce a surplus of 5.6 trillion dollars over the next ten years. His approval rating hovered around 67 percent. To be a moderate was a good thing. It showed leadership and flexibility. A politician who could cross party lines and compromise was considered reasonable. This was considered good government and good politics.

So, it was only natural that Bush would try the same technique. He wanted to show that he was not some rigid hard ass. He wanted to make it clear he was not one of those stubborn dipshit conservatives like Newt Gingrich. Gingrich proved to be no match for Clinton. He was out classed and out smarted by the Clinton machine all throughout the 1990's.

Bush had a good idea, he would try to show that he was a different type of conservative. He would show that he's a "compassionate conservative." He wanted to cast himself as the Republican version of Clinton. Someone who could govern from the center while still not selling out on certain core beliefs. This was not just a good idea, but it worked. Bush eked out a close victory over Al Gore to become president.

George W. Bush walked into a pretty good situation for the most part. Despite a recession from the dot-com bubble bursting, unemployment was still pretty low, and Clinton's budget was on track to produce an annual 230 billion dollar surplus.

So what's a president to do when looking for something to fix? How about start breaking things first.

Bush wasted no time wiping out Clinton's annual surplus. In his first year in office, Bush came with huge tax cut packages. The tax cuts greatly helped upper income Americans. In fact, studies by the Tax Policy Center showed that the bottom 60 percent of Americans received only 13.7 percent of the tax cuts. So it was a great idea by Bush. Give huge tax breaks, in the middle of recession, to people who don't really need tax breaks. Of course, I am being a smartass. You see, somehow the money is going to trickle down to the rest of us. Yeah right!!! But more on that later.

Now the tax cuts were not paid for because tax cuts (tax cuts for the rich that is) pay for themselves. At least according to conservatives they do. This was a reversal from a strange and backward policy instituted by Bill Clinton. Clinton enforced something called PAYGO. It meant government had to actually (gasp) act like normal people and pay for what it wanted.

If government wanted to pass a bill to fund a war that costs 100 billion dollars, it would have to cut 100 billion from somewhere else or raise taxes by 100 billion, or a mixture of both. That war, pet project, or whatever had to be paid for. Apparently this strange method is one of the reasons the country had a balanced budget for four straight years.

Bush being the savvy economist that he was, quickly saw the nonsense in Clinton's scheme. Having to pay for stuff is a nagging inconvenience that no president or Congress should have to endure. So Bush quickly got to work and wiped out that stupid surplus. Why should government have to live within its means when it can borrow money from China whenever it wants? Even Dick Chaney flexed his intellectual muscle when he openly admitted that, "deficits don't matter."

So the largest surplus in U.S. history went down the toilet rather quickly. Rich people however, thought it was pretty hilarious that they just received huge tax breaks that were never even lobbied for. George W. Bush was pretty happy too, and he wouldn't stop there.

After the terrorist attacks of September 11, Bush rightly waged war on Afghanistan. The U.S. invasion toppled the Taliban. This war was of necessity. There was only one problem. Bush didn't bother to finance the war. Once again, being the savvy economist that he is, Bush realized that although waging war was a necessity, paying for it was not. Maybe he thought of the war the way he thought about those tax cuts. Somehow it would pay for itself. Who knows? What we do know is that the Bush spending spree was just getting started.

With huge tax breaks for the rich doing nothing to spark the economy and a suddenly mounting deficit that didn't exist a few years prior to his administration, Bush had to do something. He would…pass a job bill, right? No, no, he would pass a plan to chip away at the deficits he caused and put the nation back on the sound fiscal footing it was on before he came into office, right? Nope, no deficit reduction plan.

So, what did a president do with such nagging problems facing the country? That's right, you guessed it, just go invade another country! And for kicks don't pay for that either! Now we're talking! What bold leadership, huh? At this point Bush had to be realizing what a great gig he had. Being president was really easy. You buy whatever you want without paying for it and then you start a war just because it seems like a really cool idea.

Of course Bush thought Iraq had weapons of mass destruction. The Bush Administration did a thorough investigation and gathered credible intelligence from a guy they *never met* named "Curveball". They knew the information was credible because...they just knew okay?! Besides, Saddam Hussein was an asshole. Why not kick his ass while everybody was still in the mood?

Somehow while pouring resources into Iraq, Bush forgot we were still in Afghanistan. A common mistake when you're fighting too many wars at once.

Another signature moment for Bush came when he signed into law the Medicare Prescription Drug, Improvement, and Modernization Act. This law cost around 400 billion dollars and you guessed it, it was not paid for!

So, the first term of President Bush was impressive to say the least. The economy that boomed under his predecessor now seemed to suck. The deficit that didn't exist prior to his administration was now over 400 billion dollars and the country was stuck in <u>two</u> wars.

So, what do you think all those small government conservatives did after Bush did such a good job of running up deficits and expanding the size of government (see Patriot Act)? Well, they re-elected him, that's what they did. After all, just because the economy was growing slower than that little midget on Fantasy Island, and the deficit had ballooned, Bush seemed to be a pretty likeable fella. And even though the money still hadn't seemed to trickle down to the other 90 percent of Americans, rich people were feeling pretty darn good about paying lower taxes. Besides, after a first term like that, how much worse could it get? It's not like he would implement policies that would help trigger the worst economic crisis in decades.

If only they knew. The walking nightmare known as George W. Bush would show that the first term was no aberration. It was, again, a glimpse of things of to come.

In his second term, it was obvious Bush was chasing a goal that alluded him in his first term. He clearly had a burning desire to convince the country that he misplaced his brain somewhere between the border of Texas, Mexico, and a state called Reality. Hurricane Katrina would be his first chance to prove it. The storm exposed just how disorganized and unprepared the Bush Administration was for a natural disaster. While victims stood on rooftops screaming for their lives, as water surrounded them, Bush strummed a guitar at a party. It seems a president's work is never done.

In 2006, with the war in Iraq turning ugly, the public seemed to have had enough. Republicans were rebuked by voters and lost control of the House and Senate. The GOP could not comprehend this moment. Didn't voters realize Saddam Hussein was an asshole?

Well, lucky for Bush he would once again have a chance to prove what a savvy economist he was. The housing market was on the verge of imploding. The deregulation process had been taking place since the Clinton era and Bush made it a point to continue it. For some reason it had failed to spur the economic growth Republicans had envisioned. Deregulating the housing market would surely give banks and mortgage companies the freedom and flexibility needed to lead people from everywhere to buy a house.

Of course, the deregulation process backfired as it always does. By 2008, the housing market would collapse and the banks were about to fail as well. The housing market collapse would lead to the worst financial crisis since the Great Depression. It was the perfect exclamation point to an absolutely failed presidency.

From two mishandled wars, to blowing the deficit to record levels, to implementing policies that led the economy straight off a cliff, to expanding the size of government more than any president in a generation, George W. Bush did it all.

I am not sure you can say he's the worst president ever, but over the last 80 years it's clear that no one president has fumbled and goofed so many things at once. Whatever George W. Bush touched, he pretty much destroyed. The irony at the end should not be lost on anyone. A Republican president institutes policies that are so devastating that he's forced to go against his own ideology and use government intervention to stop an all-out collapse of the private sector. This would be like

Ghandi having to admit his whole philosophy concerning non-violence was a sham and then he picks up a machine gun and starts mowing people down.

Some people always ask, when are you going to stop blaming Bush? Well, I will tell you when. When it's no longer his fault that's when. If my kid is killed by a drunk driver I am going to blame the drunk driver. I am not going to blame his wife for making him mad that night or blame the fact that Bud Ice beer is easy to buy. I am blaming the drunk driver. He's the jerk that got behind the wheel.

George W. Bush is the drunk driver who got behind the wheel and drove the economy straight off a cliff. That's his fault. He wanted the job, he took responsibility, and he failed miserably.

As of right now, no one is more responsible for the pain and suffering of the middle class than George W. Bush and his gang of buddies in Congress. It is an injustice to the American people to say otherwise. This is an indictment on the right wing media and phony politicians who lie to Americans in such a way. The right wing media should be charged with perjury for their recalcitrant insistence on spinning the facts while distorting the history of what actually took place. Every time they dance around the fact that Bush is responsible for today's economic hardships it is a slap in the face to every American who's out of work. This is not opinion, it's fact. I know it, these clowns at Fox News know it, along with the rest of these morons who are suddenly staunch fiscal conservatives.

Bush got everything he wanted while in office. He got deregulation, he got huge tax breaks for the rich...he got everything that supports the conservative ideology of how to make the economy grow. The Bush conservative ideology failed on several fronts while he was in office. The proof is in the stats, in the data, and was witnessed by the entire country. It's important to keep all of this in mind as we examine the current predicament of the country.

By understanding what got us into our current mess we can better understand how to get out of it and not repeat it. It's not just about Bush. By keeping it fresh in our minds that Bush is to blame we also remember the methods that were used. It's just like the example of the drunk driver. I blame him for killing my kid and then I might do my best to outlaw drunk driving. Bush is the driver and his policies should never be repeated.

The methods used by Bush are a manifestation of a warped ideology that says if you cater to the rich it will trickle down to everyone else. It's a perverse thinking that says deregulation allows the talented to move with more freedom and flexibility. This will spur an economic utopia. It's an ideology that says the elite (rich) play by their own rules and the rest of us peasants can bask a little in their glow. This ideology is a proven failure. Plain and simple. It has never worked except for that top one percent that has money to fund campaigns or pay lobbyist on Capitol Hill to represent them. For the other 99 percent of America, it's a complete myth.

So, while Fox News and that pill-popping, fat ass Rush Limbaugh dish out a bunch of horseshit because they want their favorite team to win, it's important to remember the facts. While Democrats and Republicans paint fictional pictures of their favorite sides they forget one thing. Real people are hurt. While Republicans hope the unemployment rate stays the same so that the president looks bad, the numbers represent real people who are suffering. 50 million Americans living in poverty and some asshole like Bill O'Reilly is more worried about protecting the Bush legacy. Yeah it's Bush's fault, and until the millions of out of work get the justice they deserve, and the millions living in poverty get the justice they deserve, then it's only right that we keep pointing the finger at the culprit.

We were fooled once by Mr. Bush. Shame on him. But if we are fooled again then shame on us. It's these very reasons that have caused today's conservative nuthouse. Republicans would lose control of the House and the Senate in 2006 and then lose the White House along with even more congressional seats in 2008. The conservative movement was rejected (or the ones in Congress at least). The policies of the last decade had been given an overwhelming thumbs down. The rigid conservatism of the 90's had been stepped all over by Clinton. The compassionate conservatism of the last decade wasn't shown much compassion by the voters. It was a farce. The Republican Party no longer had an ideology or a clue. The same core voters who were there for Bush during two presidential cycles had now experienced defeat.

Republicans had a choice. Face up to the fact that they failed and work with the new president or obstruct as much as possible. To be fair, the minority party always plays the role of the obstructionist, but even when Bush was in office Democrats gave it a rest sometimes. It took Democrats to help Bush pass his tax cuts: No Child Left Behind, the Medicare Prescription Drug Program, and funding for the government. You know that whole debt ceiling thing? Democrats gave Bush the needed votes to raise the debt ceiling on several occasions. Republicans, on the other hand, seem to be so shell-shocked by the beat downs they experienced in two election cycles that they were not going to give an inch. They were really pissed, but they had nothing going for them. They had no energy, no enthusiasm, no cause. All they had was Fox News and quite frankly that guy, Ann Coulter, can only influence the electorate so much. Oops, I mean girl. That *girl*, Ann Coulter. I have a tendency to mistake her for a guy. My apology to the readers for an accurate de—I mean, inaccurate description.

The obstructionist scheme to resist the president on everything started the day he came into office. Just being a sore loser and saying 'no' would not put a dent in the president's armor nor would it resurrect the conservative movement. Bush had single-handedly screwed his own party for a generation unless something miraculous happened. Well, something close to miraculous did happen. Just when it seemed all was lost after two disastrous election cycles and a walking catastrophe known as George W. Bush, fate would once again smile upon the Republican Party. It was time for a Tea Party.

2 | GETTING THE PARTY STARTED

Disillusioned Republicans were like a guy who just got dumped by his girlfriend. You know the type. He just got out of a bad relationship, so he channels all his anger like a little girl. He becomes stubborn and moody. He doesn't want to talk or compromise, he just wants to go back to the way things were. To make matters worse, he becomes jealous of the new guy who just moved into the neighborhood. His disdain for the new guy becomes creepy.

The new guy in this case is Barack Obama. A young, charismatic, popular president who has been in office less than a month when conservatives decide he's done enough damage. The start of the great movement against Barack Obama did not come from congressional Republicans. They were too busy pouting like a bunch of bitches while he passed the stimulus. Nope, it took a media outlet, and it was staged perfectly. It almost invoked memories of when Nixon would stage town hall meetings in the 1960's. Of course, no one knew they were staged until about 30 years later. That's what made them so clever. This particular staged event is what gave birth to the Tea Party. The whole setting to this propaganda campaign is actually brilliant.

February 20, 2009, the new president announces his administration has decided to go forward with the Homeowner Affordability and Stability Plan. The whole idea of the plan is to help families facing foreclosure to stay in their homes. This was deemed outrageous by many conservatives. Bailing out the banks that caused the crisis is one thing. But to bail out homeowners who were victims of the whole crisis is way too extreme. Look out for the crooks who started this mess. Anything else is unadulterated Marxism.[1]

The formal response to the president's announcement would be broadcast on CNBC. CNBC is the perfect network for the response. The network receives their ad revenue from the Financial Services Industry. Because of this fact they have no problem spewing out whatever propaganda many Wall Street banks want them to spew. CNBC is not just friends with Wall St., the network pretty much works for Wall St.[1]

The response that was broadcast on the little propaganda network came from a real, live shit-face named Rick Santelli. Rick is not just a good old conservative patriot who loves his country. Santelli is a well-known PR puppet for banks like Goldman Sachs and J.P. Morgan. CNBC (a.k.a. Wall St. employee) not only had one of "their own" to deliver the spirited rebuttal, but they even had an enthusiastic audience to root Santelli on. This hand-selected group of angry and fed up patriots was the Chicago Board of Trade. These are the same nice people who did a lot of betting on commodities like food, oil, and natural gas in the summer of 2008.[1]

They helped contribute to the huge bubble that caused all these commodities to sky rocket in value. It was not only a devastating blow to the U.S. economy, but it caused millions of people around the world to starve to death. Supply and demand was pretty much the same and had nothing to do with the huge spikes. It was a speculative bubble. That's a known fact that was admitted to by many banks.[1]

This was the hand-picked audience for the hand-picked speaker. A group of greedy assholes who just helped play a part in one of the most devastating economic bubbles ever. Of course it was huge blow to the U.S. and global economy, but they made a few bucks. All in a day's work. These were the cheering fired-up patriots in Santelli's audience. It was time to stand up to that president that wants to mess everything up his first month in office.[1] So now you see the warped cast of characters who were hand-picked to act as if they were pissed.

With this setting, the lowlife, lying scumbag Rick Santelli would stir his audience into a frenzy. He really lit into Obama saying, "Why don't you put up a website to have people vote on the internet as a referendum to see if we really want to subsidize the losers' mortgages? Or would we like to at least buy cars and buy houses in foreclosure and give them to people that might have a chance to actually prosper down the road and reward people that "carry the water" instead of "drinking the water"?"[1]

After a brief back and forth, ass-kissing session between Santelli, Joe Kernen and Rebecca Quick, Santelli would declare, "We're thinking about having a Chicago Tea Party in July. All you capitalist that want to show up to Lake Michigan, I am organizing." The hand-picked crooks, I mean crowd, went bananas. The clip was an internet sensation. It stirred the souls of conservatives and gave Republicans a rallying cry. The shot heard around the conservative spectrum was water carriers shouldn't have to pay for water drinkers. The message was simple. The new Black president with the funny name is trying to redistribute the wealth.[1]

The huge bailout for the homeowners was 75 billion dollars. This huge amount of money is what energized the conservative movement and made Rick Santelli a living legend. Yet, Santelli and the party was nowhere to be found when the Bush Administration passed a 700 billion dollar bailout program known as TARP. They were pretty silent about the other bailouts as well.[1]

Now I'm not saying that it's something personal against the new guy. It just seems a bit suspicious that the Bush Administration came with quite a few bailouts and the moment the Democrat comes with one bailout that's ten times smaller than the one they turned a blind eye to they go ape shit. Did I mention the guy had only been in office a month?

This group of patriots got organized, and by the summer of 2009 they grabbed on to healthcare. Let the Tea Party begin. The Tea Party is considered a minority of the Republican Party, but they are a noisy little group of pricks. They are a very diverse group of middle-aged White people who display rebel flags at many rallies while sporting billboards showing the president wearing white face paint with black eyes and black lips or the new Tea Party favorite: a skunk with its huge white stripe showing. The comparison is really quite creative. According to the Tea Party, the skunk and Obama have a lot in common. "They're both black with a white streak and everything about them stinks." That is a quote. They even have billboards that display our Black president as a monkey.

This, of course, is not meant to be racist. It's just some good old boys poking fun at the Negro in the White House. Those Tea Partiers, what a great sense of humor, huh? I wonder what they will do next for a laugh? Burn a cross on the White House lawn? That should really crack 'em up at the next bingo tournament. Yep, I just can't understand what all the fuss is about. If I am not mistaken they have at least two people who are Black and are considered members of the 20 million movement. Oh yeah, Herman Cain, that's one. Mr. 999 himself. Of course I am not too sure if Mr. 999 even likes black people, but to heck with it. That's proof right there the Tea Party is all good with black folks.

In the fall of 2009, the Tea Party passionately protested the healthcare bill. This scared the shit out of congressional Democrats who suddenly began to wonder if the healthcare bill was a death trap. The months of democratic wrangling and bickering behind closed doors only added fuel to the fire. Suddenly, thanks to the Tea Party, Republicans were resurrected from the dead. It was a conservative revival.

Remember the jealous creepy guy I mentioned earlier in the chapter. Well, now he found a new girlfriend. The Republicans started dating the Tea Party and fell in love overnight. The new girl realized just how much they needed her and began making a list of demands. Playing the role of the lovesick puppy who found his soul mate, Republicans aimed to please. They promised every and anything for her hand in marriage. The girl tells him he's got to change his ways. He agrees. She makes a list of unrealistic demands and he agrees again, even though he knows he can't possibly live up to all this bullshit. He signs contracts, pledges, etc...he panders to her and she keeps tightening her leash on him. Well, you get the picture.

The Tea Party began protesting against Obama's big government agenda. Their complaint for the first few months of the movement was that they had been taxed enough already. "No more taxation!", they demanded. Polls show that many Tea Party members felt Obama had been covertly raising taxes. Data shows that Americans are actually paying taxes at the lowest rate (when adjusted by inflation) since the 1950's.

To make things worse, it was somehow brought to their attention that the president gave out numerous tax breaks in the so-called stimulus package. To justify the fact that they had somehow overlooked something that everybody else knew, they explained that *if* the president continued his spending spree, taxes will eventually have to be raised. I am not making this stuff up. I couldn't if I tried.

So, it became about the government takeover of

healthcare. The second complaint was that deficits were too high. Deficits are, in fact, over a trillion dollars, as of this writing. When they realized that they didn't goof that fact up as well and deficits really were huge, the Tea Party went bananas.

Now before we go any further, the question must be asked, where were the Tea Party when the Bush Administration pushed the deficit to over a trillion dollars and stacked up a mountain of debt? Where was this intense, passionate, and determined movement? Well, you get some different answers on this. One response is that they didn't know what a deficit was. That's kind of convenient. I guess that would explain why there was no uproar when Dick Chaney boldly declared, "deficits don't matter." Another response is that they were not happy then either, but it was time to put a stop to these deficits. One can only speculate on what the Tea Party was thinking during the Bush era. The facts, however, cannot be disputed. They were not protesting or speaking up on anything. Another fact is that when Bush won re-election he won with about 85 percent of the GOP vote. These numbers indicate that many of these Tea Party members were too busy re-electing Bush to worry about his spending spree. We don't have to mention his huge expansion of government (see: The Patriot Act, No Child Left Behind, and the Medicare Prescription Drug Program). Well if not then, why now? Why the fever pitch intensity today? Maybe it's because Bush did a lot for the rich. (Remember those tax breaks?) He wasn't bailing out those lazy homeowners either. The ones who just want to drink the water. Nope, he was looking out for the ones that had spilled the water on everyone else. A real capitalist that Bush is.

So, will we ever know? Of course we will, and the evidence is right there. Based on the facts it's obvious Tea Party members supported George W. Bush in his bid for re-election. Despite his big government agenda and his wild spending spree. It's only after Republicans lost power in Congress that the conservative movement went crazy over big government and big deficits. It was only after the 2008 elections that we saw this spirited movement which refused to be dissuaded and silenced. This new scion of Reaganism would tenaciously stand up to big government and big spending. Suddenly, these staunch fiscal conservatives demanded to be heard. So, why now?

The Tea Party Movement is not just angry about deficits or some lack of respect for the Constitution. If that were the case they would have been beating down the door to the White House several years ago to challenge Bush to a steel cage match. They are angry because the Tea Party is just another name for the Republican Party. They are not some non-partisan movement that hates tyranny. They are pissed because they got pummeled for two straight election cycles and in the process they lost their sense of identity.

Compassionate conservatism was a flop, and the conservative movement of the 90's was more feasible, but it was lacking something. So the mission became simple. Take the brand of conservatism of the 90's and push it even more to the right. Make it more extreme and more militant. Why, you might ask? Because as rigid as that form of conservatism was, it wasn't enough to win back the White House in 1996. Republicans felt Newt Gingrich had the right idea. He led conservatives to a historical win in 1994 when they took control over the House for the first time in 40 years. But he wasn't conservative enough. He wasn't disciplined or militant enough. In their mind, had Newt Gingrich possessed those attributes then conservatives would have won the culture war of the 90's. Newt was a letdown to them. Instead of dialing it up, Bush seemed to be dialing it down.

The last time Republicans possessed a consistent presence in the White House that didn't end in disgrace or defeat was the Reagan era. Reagan's actions never matched his rhetoric. To listen to him tell it, he was anti-establishment, anti-spending, anti-etc., etc. Reagan quickly learned that type of ideology makes for great sound bites on a campaign trail, but doesn't actually match the reality of governing a superpower.

It was, however, this type of conservative—in the minds of the Tea Party—that kept Republicans in power. This is the real reason why Reagan is the icon of the Republicans. It's not *because* of his actions. It's *despite* his actions he was still a winner. His actions show he violated many articles of faith that conservatives cling to.

He was the last real winner Republicans had. And why did he win? Because he campaigned as a staunch conservative ideologue. His words were more powerful than his actions ever were.

This is why Republicans run from Reagan's record and pretend like he never raised taxes or gave a path to citizenship for illegal immigrants. His record would blemish the image conservatives painted for him. It's really a fictional character who leads the charge of the conservative movement as their superhero. He held onto the White House and cemented his legacy by being a right wing extremist who stood up to the evil liberals. With charming alacrity he used an amazing bravura to descry the issues facing the country and lead us all out of darkness. After the dark night the sun would rise and the bright light would signal that it's "Morning in America".

So, the goal is to be like Reagan and win the fight. How do you do that? Right wing extremism. George H.W. Bush would only reinforce this idea. He won the White House after Reagan's second term and decided to be a moderate and govern from the center. This was the same Bush who campaigned like a staunch conservative. He's the same Bush that assailed Senator Bob Dole in the New Hampshire Primary of 1988. Dole refused to rule out tax increases in a deficit reduction plan of any kind. Stupid Bob Dole, he had the audacity to be honest and sensible. Bush, of course, had the famous "read my lips, no new taxes" platform. Once again rhetoric didn't match reality. Bush had promised to get the deficit left by Reagan under 50 billion dollars without raising taxes. Maybe he just wasn't very good at math. Bush ended up raising taxes and still left behind a 350 billion dollar deficit.

The economy was a mess all throughout his term. He ended up losing his bid for re-election.

The main reason George H.W. Bush lost re-election was the economy. Had he won re-election, Republicans would still be praising him and would act like he never raised taxes. After all, this is the method they use when they glorify Reagan who pretty much governed like he lost his mind and raised taxes 11 times. Reagan was a winner. Bush Sr. was a loser. In their minds, there is only one explanation for his loss. He was a stupid liberal Republican who should have embraced his conservative roots. Had he been more conservative the economy would have been better. The only way to prosper is to understand the true traditions of America. Conservatism.

Then good ole slick Willie came along. Bill Clinton won the White House in 1992 and Democrats held the majority in both the Senate and the House. For the first time in 12 years, Republicans did not rule the White House. They were reeling from the defeat, and when Republicans are reeling from defeat they do a great job of flexing their bold, unabashed insanity streak. It usually works too. They all seem to transform as they channel their inner Barry Goldwater. This would have to take place to make up for the colossal screw up, George H.W. Bush. Lucky for them, Bill Clinton was one big colossal screw up his first two years in office, and his moronic clumsiness gave Republicans a lifeline.

The Brady Bill already had conservatives fuming, but it was healthcare that reenergized them. President Clinton put the first lady in charge of a task force to come up with a plan to overhaul the nation's healthcare system. Conservatives saw their moment and quickly pounced on it. Led by such characters as Newt Gingrich, Rush Limbaugh, the insurance companies, and the tobacco companies, conservatives launched an all-out propaganda war against the bill. The tactics scared congressional Democrats and the fiasco was a huge embarrassment to President Clinton. At this point, Republicans had the momentum and refused to relinquish it.

Clinton's budget was extremely helpful to the economy[2], but he allowed Republicans to control the public narrative. Republicans reminded the public over and over about the tax increases in the bill. Scandals were also popping up everywhere. Allegations of his involvement in fraudulent dealings with Madison Savings began to surface. The White Water River Real Estate scandal seemed to be following him everywhere.[2]

Then in June of 1993, there was the now legendary "Hair Force One" moment. The president was kicked back on Air Force One while getting a 200 dollar haircut. The plane he's on while receiving this immaculate piece of work on his head is shutting down two runways at once at Los Angeles International Airport for one hour. How's that for looking out of touch with mainstream America?

In July of that same year, there was the mysterious suicide of Vincent Foster, a top White House aide. Rumor circulated that he died somewhere other than where the body was found.[2] The so-called experts who put the rumor in the air never produced a really good clue much less facts to this theory. But, in politics, rumors are sometimes all that's needed.

In October of 1993, there was a public outrage over a humanitarian mission to Somalia that turned into an absolute debacle of epic proportions. An ambush took place that resulted in eighteen U.S. soldiers being killed while 78 others were injured. The incident became known as Black Hawk Down. It was a political nightmare for Clinton. It brought back memories of Jimmy Carter's failed attempt to rescue the hostages from Iran in 1979. Jimmy Carter had good intentions and had the hostages been rescued he would have campaigned for re-election as a hero. Instead the mission failed. The rescue choppers crashed and Carter looked both weak and incompetent. Clinton, at this point, was looking a lot like Carter; a weak one term president. The only difference was that Clinton had a mountain of scandals at his doorstep.[2]

In May of 1994, a lawsuit was filed by Paula Jones against the president for sexual harassment. Election season was heating up and Democratic candidates were being told to distance themselves from Clinton to the point of acting like he had the bubonic plague.[2]

Right before the election some of Clinton's top aides began to resign because of scandals. All the sideshows that contributed to the Clinton circus for the first two years culminated in one of the most lopsided defeats ever experienced by one party in a single election cycle. Democrats would lose 52 House seats and 8 Senate seats.[2]

It was a stunning collapse for the Democrats. Not since the 1930's had one party lost so many seats in one election. It was an undisputed rebuke of Bill Clinton. And it was a rebuke with historical significance. For the first time in 40 years, Democrats no longer were the majority party in the House of Representatives. The man who was looked at as the chief culprit for this meltdown was Bill

Clinton himself.

Republicans smelled blood and knew the White House was next. The man who was viewed as the architect behind this new conservative revolution was Newt Gingrich. Clinton's troubles are what really gave Newt all the ammo he needed. Newt put together the "Contract with America" and would be voted Speaker of the House. Conservatives felt he resurrected the conservative movement from the dead. Newt—unlike George H.W. Bush—pushed hard to the right and fed into the theory that extreme right wing is the only way to win.

The reality of the situation is Newt Gingrich never was as brilliant as he thought he was and the Conservative Revolution was really propelled by Clinton's own shortcomings. For years, conservatives have showered praise on Newt for being the driving force behind the House takeover of 1994. But the facts are clear.

Newt Gingrich didn't need to do anything. Republicans had the luxury of sitting back and watching the show. It was obvious Bill Clinton could not get out of his own way.

Nevertheless, seizing control of the House was a huge accomplishment and it clearly set the stage. A Republican controlled Congress vs. a weakened Democratic president in the White House. Bill Clinton's approval rating was in the low 40's and his legal troubles were still mounting.

Gingrich and his band of idiots would continue the strategy of the first two years which was not really a strategy at all. Continue to obstruct, act ultra conservative, don't compromise and do whatever the pill-popper Rush Limbaugh said. That strategy worked because they were the minority party. They controlled Congress now. Instead of trying to govern and adapt to their new role, Republicans decided to go in for the kill, every chance of everyday. This reckless greed for power would lead to a tactical mistake by Newt Gingrich. It's a mistake that has haunted Republicans for years.

In November of 1995, Bill Clinton would hold his ground on some hot button issues. Republicans would pick a fight and shut the government down. Clinton didn't blink. Despite the fact that they controlled Congress, Republicans didn't seem to understand that they did not control the White House. The GOP decided to ram a budget straight through the White House door. They wanted to use their budget to reform Medicare and dozens of other programs while cutting taxes—mostly for the rich.

The amendments in their budgets were a bit far reaching to say the least. They included: limiting appeals by death row inmates, make it harder to issue health, safety and environmental regulations, and commit the president to a seven year balanced budget. The real kicker was raising premiums by over $10.00 a month on Medicare Part B. Now imagine that. Cut taxes for the rich, but take out of the pockets of senior citizens.

Bill Clinton called Newt Gingrich's bluff. When Newt began his journey to Stupidville he didn't bother to take a few things into account. His ideologue driven budget might not be too popular and despite two years of goof-ups Clinton just might be a very savvy politician if given the right opportunity.

Sensing a defeat, Newt made things worse for Republicans. He began to open his mouth about being snubbed by Clinton on a return flight from Israel the previous week. As the Washington Post reported on November 17, 1995, "This is petty", he told reporters, "You land at Andrews (Air Force Base) and you've been on the plan 25 hours and nobody has talked to you and they just ask you to get off the plane by the back ramp...you just wonder, where is the sense of courtesy, where is the sense of manners?" Poor Newt. It sounds to me like the guy just needed a hug. It should be a good thing when a guy gets in touch with his sensitive side. Even if it's really sensitive, like four years old and still in need of a good stiff shot of breast milk sensitive.

The remarks produced a real whirlwind of protest from Democrats. The White House would pour it on by releasing a photo that shows Clinton and Gingrich talking during the flight. Headlines from the Daily News read:

CRYBABY!!! NEWT'S TANTRUM!!!
He closed down the government because Clinton
made him sit at back of plane!

While Gingrich began to implode, Clinton maneuvered with a nimble dexterity and political savvy that seemed to catch Republicans off guard.

Polls showed Americans sided with Clinton 51-24 percent. Some polls showed wider margins than that.

Republicans were forced to surrender. Clinton's win would reinforce his nickname, "The Comeback Kid". Republicans gave him a chance and he took full advantage of it. Clinton's presidency would never be the same. It seemed like whenever he would butt heads with Republicans from that moment on he would manage to come out ahead. Newt usually led the charge and usually suffered the most devastating consequences. It started to become obvious that Newt Gingrich was no match for Clinton. He became Clinton's foil.

Clinton's first term would wind down with a few big legislative victories. The biggest one of all was probably welfare reform. Clinton had refashioned himself as a moderate and governed from the center. He positioned himself as a solid leader and the voice of reason against an extremist right wing faction. Clinton cruised to re-election.

In his second term, Clinton would be impeached by the House of Representatives for perjury, but the Senate did not have the needed votes. This one last fight would cost Newt Gingrich his spot as House Speaker. The public was fed up with him. Republicans had followed Newt into several Clinton traps. They'd had enough. Newt was kicked to the curb. Clinton would finish out his second term with a robust economy and four straight balanced budgets. The biggest slap in the face to Republicans was despite all the scandals and controversy, Clinton came from under all his troubles unscathed and left office as one of the most popular presidents in U.S. history.

Clinton had single-handedly stepped all over the conservative movement of the 90's and exposed Newt

Gingrich to be a real dipshit moron who had never produced a shred of evidence that he was really as smart as people gave him credit for. The final poke in the eye would come a few years after Clinton's second term was finished. It was revealed that while Newt Gingrich was pushing for Clinton's impeachment for allegedly lying about the Monica Lewinsky affair, that he (Gingrich) was having an affair with his secretary. Bill Clinton had to be doubled over with laughter. What a brilliant ending to such a one-sided beat down. Hollywood could not have dreamed up a better script.

For anyone to claim that Newt Gingrich was brilliant or had some type of fantastic career is absurd. All he did was lead a radical faction into consistent beat downs at the hands of Clinton and then the punch-drunk party punched him right out of the door. They stripped him out of his speakership and said thanks for making us all look stupid, now get out.

Clinton forced Republicans to compromise on key issues and then took credit for legislative victories.

It's important to understand that this isn't the first time Republicans went nuts and it's not the first time a Democrat in the White House used them to be his foil for re-election. In the late 1940's, Republicans took control of the House of Representatives. Realizing how unpopular Harry Truman was at the time, Republicans continued to obstruct figuring the White House was next. Truman decided to campaign against "the do-nothing Congress", picking a fight with them every chance he got. He used Republicans as his ticket to re-election.

Wanting to keep the tradition of serving only two terms, Truman decided not to run for President again. He'd spent almost eight years in the White House, but the first half of the time he spent as president was actually finishing out the fourth term of F.D.R.'s presidency after his unexpected death. His successor, Dwight D. Eisenhower, was being pursued for the Democratic nomination just a few years prior to becoming a Republican presidential hopeful in 1952. Eisenhower withdrew his name from consideration for the Democratic nomination in 1948. He would become the first Republican to sit in the White House in two decades.

The fact that Eisenhower had only been a Republican for a few years explains why he came across as so sensible. He was not chained to the conservative ideology. He did not feel hell bent on pandering to his conservative base. He was a moderate who worked well with the House Democrats. These are some of the main reasons he had such crossover appeal with many Democratic voters. Conservatives didn't mind this one bit. As long as a Republican was in the White House, they were happy. That dream was stolen however, in the 1960 election.

Richard Nixon was no Dwight Eisenhower and he would lose an extremely close race to John F. Kennedy. For a moment, it seemed voters as a whole had found a president that both sides could fall in love with. After a few years it started to become clear that J.F.K. had swept America off her feet. Then tragedy would strike. John F. Kennedy would be assassinated on November 22, 1963. Lyndon B. Johnson would be sworn in. With just a year to go until the elections, Johnson would begin implementing the war on poverty and then would sign into law the Civil Rights Act of 1964. It was clear that L.B.J. was the favorite in the 1964 election. He would be looked at as the guy to carry out the agenda of John F. Kennedy while having the ability to improvise as needed.

Conservatives knew a "normal" candidate wasn't going to just steal the election from L.B.J. They figured they would need someone who's not just conservative, but who's an ideologue who's dead set on putting the conservative agenda front and center. That someone would be Barry M. Goldwater.

Barry Goldwater was the type of clown that only half the circus could love, but everybody seemed to enjoy the spectacle he made of himself.

He was a Republican from Arizona. He was pretty successful in the business world. After finding a trading post that would grow into a chain of department stores he would become president of Goldwaters, Inc. He would write a book in 1960 called "The Conscience of a Conservative" and emerged as a real champion of the right wing Republican Party.[2] He was everything a wing nut could love. He wanted a sharp reduction in the size of government, repeal of the income tax, an end to federal aid in education, a voluntary form of social security, and was one of many Republicans to vote against the Civil Rights Act of 1964. His views were disturbing to establishment Republicans like Dwight Eisenhower, but the conservatives in the party loved him. And when the right-wing-wing nuts love someone, other Republicans follow along. This theory of having to push to the extreme was slapped in the face and turned on its head.

Lyndon B. Johnson destroyed Barry Goldwater in the election carrying 44 states and winning 61 percent of the popular vote. Goldwater would carry just five deep south states and his home state of Arizona. Republicans lost huge numbers of seats across the country as well. The Barry Goldwater experiment was a colossal failure that reverberated from the national elections all the way to local elections across the country.

It's important to keep these pieces of history in mind for a few reasons. The first, conservatives have a history of becoming radical when they are trying to regain power. And secondly, their radical agenda is always used as a weapon against them by their democratic opponents.

After the Goldwater experiment, conservatives didn't mind supporting a candidate who seemed a little more flexible than Goldwater. You know, the type who could actually get elected. Richard Nixon seemed to fit that category. He had broad support from the moderates in the party. Being a moderate was cool again. Not just because Nixon won the election, but he also won re-election. Then in the middle of his second term, the Watergate scandal really caught fire and when it did it burned the White House down. Being a moderate sucked all over again. Stupid Nixon, that's what he gets for being a moderate. This sort of warped thinking on the grass roots level is what has the Republican Party pulling itself apart at the seams right now.

On August 9, 1974, Richard Nixon resigned in

disgrace. In his farewell address he said, "To continue to fight though the months ahead for my personal vindication would almost totally absorb the time and attention of both the president and the Congress in a period when our entire focus should be on the great issues of peace abroad and prosperity without inflation at home."[2]

Translation:
There's no point in me going through this any longer and I know damn well that I'm guilty and you know damn well that I'm guilty. If I stay, everybody's going to be focused on the fact that I am full of shit and I am not going to be able to get anything done or divert attention from myself in any way, so I am getting the hell out of here.

If that wasn't enough to disgrace the Republican Party then Gerald Ford would make sure there was more to come. Ford was sworn in on August 9, 1974. The same day Nixon resigned of course. In September of 1974, Ford granted Nixon a full pardon for *everything*. That pretty much covered it. The pardon, of course, drew a fire storm of protests. Even Ford's press secretary, Jerald F. terHorst, resigned in protest. Talk about a backlash.[2]

Everything about Ford's presidency seemed to be a failure. Even his "Whip Inflation Now" campaign went up in smoke. Also known as "WIN", the campaign was launched with a lot of fanfare. They even had cute little WIN buttons. Unfortunately for Ford and the rest of the country, WIN turned out to be a loss. The campaign was abandoned as other measures had to be taken to combat the recession of 1974-75.

With Ford trailing Jimmy Carter in the polls, conservatives knew they were facing the prospect of defeat. As usual the conservatives in the party went into freak out mode and split the party. Barry Goldwater was not the face of the movement this time. On this occasion it was the former Governor of California, Ronald Reagan. He had defeated Ford in some key states during the primaries. North Carolina, Texas, and Indiana are not states that an incumbent president is supposed to lose in a bid for the party nomination. At the Republican National Convention, Ford managed to hold off Reagan and his movement by only 60 delegates. The spectacle of almost losing the nomination was an embarrassment in itself. No incumbent president lost his party's nomination in the 20th century. That should give you an idea of how bad this looked. In fact the last incumbent president to lose the party's nomination was Andrew Johnson back in 1868.

Ironically, Ford survived Reaganites thanks to a key endorsement from none other than Barry Goldwater. You remember, Mr. Super Ultra-Conservative. He endorsed the moderate over the ultra-conservative Reagan. The same Reagan that campaigned for Mr. Goldwater in the 1964 election. He didn't want Reagan to win in 1976. Extreme right didn't seem to be working. The last two Republicans to win the White House were Eisenhower and Nixon up until that point. Both were moderates. Ford was a moderate. It was best to go with the odds. The odds were in favor of the moderate. Once again, it was not about core convictions or who the best candidate was. It was all about winning back the White House. It was all about having a Republican in power, that's it. Reaganites followed suit, but if things didn't go well for Ford they knew they would have to try a new strategy.

Jimmy Carter would defeat Ford. His one term as president was one long snake bitten slog. Runaway inflation, a gasoline shortage, a sluggish economy, and the Iranian Hostage Debacle were too many issues at once for Carter to overcome. Americans had clearly lost confidence in his administration. He seemed unable to impose his will on a Democratic Congress and unable to have any type of influence abroad. With a shoddy record and the economy in disarray, Carter tried to keep the focus on Reagan. It was the old "I might be a moron, but this guy is a moron **and** a jerk" strategy. This innovative technique backfired. Republicans found documents listing 660 promises Carter made during his campaign against Gerald Ford. Then they compared the promises to what he actually accomplished. Much to their delight it seemed Carter thought he was campaigning for another candidate or thought he was campaigning for another country. Whatever the case, it sure looked like he was trying not to do what he promised.

Carter made some unrealistic promises that could not have been kept if he would have magically turned his four year term into a scene from Groundhog Day and began reliving the first year in office for about a decade. One of the most ridiculous promises he made was to trim the inflation rate to four percent while the cost of living was rising by double digits. He failed to balance the budget and increased defense spending after saying he wouldn't. Both of the issues turned into broken promises. So to make matters worse, now the perception of Carter was not just about someone who was incompetent, but also a liar.

The conservative movement was energized and ready to take back power, and take back the party. There would be no issue about a moderate this time. Ronald Reagan would be the candidate to do it. It was time to push hard to the right. It didn't work for Barry Goldwater against Lyndon B. Johnson, but let's face it, Jimmy Carter was no L.B.J. Besides, being a moderate was clearly out of style, just ask Ford. It was time to try the extreme radical wing nut tactics again.

Reagan's platform would reshape even the mainstream structure of the party for years to come. He wanted to drop the party's long standing support for an Equal Rights Amendment for Women: He wanted steep tax cuts, a balanced budget, greater defense spending, and a constitutional ban on abortion just to name a few. Unlike Barry Goldwater, Reagan won. The country was reeling and needed a change. Conservatives had found their voice through Reagan and he was now the face of the movement. Extreme right wing tactics won back the White House.

So as you can see, Republicans have been suffering from extremism for years. What happened in the 1990's was nothing new. What makes the Conservative Revolution of the 90's so relevant is that many of those same conservatives are the ones who watched Reagan raise taxes and still blow holes in the deficit and applauded him while doing it. Then they used his rhetoric to turn militant when they lost the White House. Unlike Reagan, they were not smart enough to adapt when they regained some level of power.

They were Reaganites though. They propelled him to power and once he was in they enjoyed every minute of it. Once a Republican was out of the White House they went ape shit again. They are the same conservatives who got behind George W. Bush and after watching him blow up the size of government they re-elected him. And they are the same radical group of Republicans that oppose Barack Obama with a religious intensity.

This is what their movement is all about. They are like a bunch of spoiled children who cry out and go into episodes of Weirdville when they are not in power. This is their country. Reagan gave them that. Bush cost them that and now by imposing their will in a similar way to 1976 they are making the establishment follow their lead. Obstruct at all times. Don't compromise, and fight the Democrat tooth and nail in hopes he will somehow just decide to pack his stuff and leave the White House on his own. The Tea Party holds Reagan in power. They are the same group that is scarred by the Nixon fiasco and the Ford debacle. Two wishy-washy moderates who fumbled the ball. Reagan displayed the attributes of a wing nut and he was a winner by doing so. They used the same grass roots tactics in the 90's but lost because Newt Gingrich failed to observe that once Reagan got in power he was able to adapt. Newt, like the rest of the wing nuts thought the envelope should be pushed even after the fight was won. This is why the Reaganites changed their tune again and got behind the moderate George W. Bush. Even after Bush had a lousy first term, they re-elected him. They were silent on his bailouts and acted like they had no idea he increased spending levels to historical proportions. And this is why they began a movement against Obama a few weeks after he got into office.

They pretend to be against tyranny and they pretend to be lovers of the Constitution, but in reality they are just a group of old school Republicans who believe their team is supposed to be running the show. To hell with the good of the country. Who cares if the auto bailout worked? It wasn't done by a Republican so it's a failure. Who cares if the Bush policies are responsible for today's hardships? The new guy had a few weeks to get it right and he didn't. Any Republican who even looks like he's trying to work with Democrats—act like a moderate—would be chastised by the Tea Party.

Republicans are now dismissive of the legitimacy of its political opposition. Conventional understanding has been tossed to the side. Evidence and facts are to be ignored. Compromise is for the weak. This is not about governing or moving the country forward. It's about winning a game. It's about doing everything possible to put your team in power. To hell with the ordinary Americans who have become collateral damage to this nonsense. It's all about regaining power at any cost. Radical right seems to be the only thing that wins. Nothing else matters.

3 | CONSERVATIVES HAVE ALWAYS BEEN LOSERS

It's really important to be fair and consider all options before we jump to conclusions about the Tea Party. As seen in the last chapter, it's pretty clear what the Tea Party is all about , but for the sake of fairness it's good to explore all our options. After all, I wouldn't want to come across as biased. Why would I be biased against a group of people who not only add to the problems in Washington when they don't get their way, but almost influence a huge economic collapse in the process (see Debt Ceiling debate in July-August of 2011)? So what if millions of Americans would have been hurt by the economic hardships that followed? Is that more important than a group of idiots trying to force a radical agenda? Those Tea Party Patriots, what's not to love?

Anyway, if the Tea Party is not just a bunch of selfish douchebags who only have power as their main objective who are they and what are they after? We could try to give them the benefit of the doubt. After all, that's what the so called liberal media does. CNN, ABC, etc…practically kiss the Tea Party's ass just so they won't be labeled "liberal media". So, let's give the Tea Party the benefit of the doubt and weigh our options. The first option is that they are really a bunch of racist bastards who hate the idea that the president of the United States is Black. There is a strong case to be made for this option. As mentioned earlier, many of the billboards displayed at Tea Party rallies had serious racial overtones. Many members claim that they had nothing to do with these billboards yet they refuse to speak out about them. Why would you want to participate in an event that displayed any type of racism? Better yet, why would you want the same moniker of an organization that displayed any type of racism?

Instead of condemning these acts, Tea Party members across the country choose not to speak out. The Tea Party has no one leader and are divided into different factions across the country. So whenever one group does something that gets negative publicity then the others can just claim: "That's them, not us." This is rather convenient. Yet they are all in lockstep together whenever it comes to everything else. They are connected by the internet and in constant communication with each other. They come from all over just to hold one rally in one particular state or city. They were in agreement for the 2010 mid-term elections. They were in agreement with each other when they begged for a government shutdown or when they all spoke out against raising the debt ceiling. The Reaganites, I mean Republicans, I mean the Tea Party act as if they are all sharing a brain, except when they dummy up on the issue of race. Then, of course, there is the rebel flags. Imagine that for a moment. Waving a rebel flag to protest against a Black president. The rebel flag should be a reminder that the South was more concerned about economics than human rights. This would be like waving a swastika to protest a Jewish president who happens to be a descendant of Holocaust victims.

I get it, the rebel flag is a symbol of how the South stood up to the North for state's rights. Yep, the right to own human beings seems like a real noble cause. The states had a right to own their own slaves, separate them from family members, beat, and degrade them. Strip a human being from the dignity and the right to feel human. Yeah, that was a real noble cause. If this is not a warped and demented sense of logic then Charles Manson should be able to run for Congress and Charlie Sheen should become the new U.S. Ambassador to Saudi Arabia on issues concerning women's rights.

If the Tea Party by some strange coincidence did not mean this to be racist then they should have had a clue that it would be taken that way. They just didn't care. That's their right, of course. Then again, wanting to wave a rebel flag anywhere at any time gives you an idea of where these people stand and what their world view is.

So, the billboards and the rebel flags are one thing. The second piece of evidence tends to lend even more weight to this theory.

The Tea Party's arguments against the president have been a bit strange to say the least. First, they claimed he was raising taxes, but that turned out to be false. Then they are upset that he's stacking massive amounts of debt. Yet, even their own party admits that the budget won't be balanced in the next decade or two decades for that matter. They are upset about the fact that he's not whacking 300 or 400 billion dollars off the deficit every year, but even their own budget guru, Paul Ryan, admits that is not possible without doing serious damage to a fragile economy.

The Obama bailouts pretty much mirror the Bush bailouts except Obama's bailouts have been a little smaller. When Bush passed TARP along with other huge slush funds for corporations that probably didn't need the money, there was no protest whatsoever. The one argument that seemed legitimate was the one against the healthcare bill. But even that seemed a bit odd at times. One of their main complaints against the bill was that it would create death panels. Which was not true, and even some Republicans admitted that was pushing it a bit far. Another complaint is that it would gut Medicare which was not true either. The Tea Party, however, protested fervently and let it be known that they wanted government to keep their hands off their Medicare. Which is hilarious since Medicare is a government run program, but polls show that the Tea Party doesn't seem to know the difference.

Yet, when Republican Congressman, Paul Ryan introduced a budget in April of 2011 to turn Medicare into a voucher program, you didn't hear a peep from the Tea Party. Democrats and independents went ballistic. Republicans/Tea Party members not only stayed silent, but they began hoping that he (Ryan) would run for president.

Had Obama introduced a plan to dismantle Medicare and turn it into a voucher program, the Tea Party would have torn their clothes off, wrapped themselves in rebel flags, and ran through the streets of Washington D.C. screaming: Freedom!!! Then they would have probably demanded a recall election that night. In short, all hell would have broken out.

Yet, when Paul Ryan does it they want him to run for president. Even as of this writing, they (the Tea Party) are hoping he gets picked on the ticket to run as vice president.

It is no doubt suspicious when some White middle-aged voters band together to oppose things that they once had no problem with. It's even more suspicious when the things they suddenly have an intense hatred for are being proposed by a Black president . Their sudden passion against the Black president for expanding the size of government would be admirable if that same passion would have been directed at George W. Bush when he was expanding the size of government. But it wasn't. Nope, it wasn't until the Black guy came along that a really, really small government became vogue.

So, what's the verdict? Is this option more feasible than the one in the last chapter? Is this the true motive of the Tea Party? The answer is no. As viable as this option might seem, it's not quite that simple. First of all, to say all the Tea Party members are a bunch of racist, bigot, assholes would be wrong. I can't honestly say that. Even though there is some evidence that a huge portion of them are. Probably 70-75 percent of them, but it's hard to get a clean 100 percent. All of them could be considered co-conspirators to the racist displays at their rallies but it's still extremely debatable.

I am convinced as I stated in the last chapter that it's all about power. I don't think race is the sole motive or the main motive. The reason it's so easy to think that the Tea Party is motivated by racism is because the Republican Party has always demonstrated racist tendencies. 90 percent of Republicans are White. Their staunch small government ideology has been a hindrance to Black people on many issues. The government intervention that conservatives oppose is what gave Black people the Civil Rights Act of 1965. Many conservatives then and now feel that the government went too far. They claim to love Dr. Martin Luther King, Jr., but it was Dr. King who pushed for government to step in. Republicans claim to not be racist but refused to lift a finger to help Blacks because doing so would interfere with their own rigid ideology. The irony of this is government intervention is what ended slavery and it was a Republican president that called for such intervention. In fact, that's what the Republican Party stood for at the time and it was that cause that it actually rallied around upon its birth.

The Republican Party was started in 1854 as the party of anti-slavery, small farmers, workers, and trades people in the West and Midwest. This had also been the Free-Soil Movement. These people were opposed to slavery and for a few reasons. The first was they were Christians. Secondly, because there was no way in hell they could compete with crops grown or goods that were produced by slave labor.[3]

Northeastern abolitionists also joined the Republicans for moral reasons. When the party did finally come into power it was joined by some of America's emerging industrial capitalist and financiers. These captains of industry didn't care about slavery one way or the other, but they supported Republicans in the Civil War because there was money to be made. They ramped up production of cannons, rifles, wagons, ships, etc...[3]

The liberal Republican president who used federal might was Abraham Lincoln, the first Republican president. Democrats were the conservatives at the time and claimed the federal government had no authority to intrude on state's rights under the 10th Amendment. All you constitutionalist out there should love this argument. Even when it comes to owning human beings states should have a right to do so. How can one possibly transgress against the vision of the founding fathers?

At the end of the war a debate was already underway concerning post war reconstruction policy. One part of the debate was between Democrats and Republicans concerning the punishment of the White rebels in the South. The other part of the debate took place within the Republican Party. They were trying to figure out just what kind of society could be created in the South and what kind of economy could be built.[3]

The Republican Party had also become a national party made up of different factions. The differences between these factions began to surface after the war. The old free-soilers and abolishers came to be called the Radical Republicans. They wanted to break up the southern plantations. With their plantation system still intact they knew slavery would just continue, but under a different name. They called for the federal government to confiscate these lands and redistribute them to poor Blacks and Whites. This didn't happen. Reconstruction was not really concerned with racial equality. It was about free labor that could be mediated through the market. Yet it had a positive impact in some ways. An alliance would be formed between freed slaves and poor Whites in the post-war South. The South remained under federal occupation for 11 years.[3]

During this time the 13th, 14th, and 15th Amendments were passed. These amendments officially abolished slavery and granted former slaves citizenship rights. It seemed action was finally being taken and Republicans were leading the charge. Congress would pass a number of laws during this period granting the basic civil rights of African-Americans, and in the process established the Freedmen's Bureau. This bureau was created to meet particular needs of former slaves. Black people were allowed to vote or run for office. Amazingly, many became state legislators, congressmen, sheriffs, and even mayors. All over the deep south Black people were beginning to hold prominent positions. The South was coming into its own, even the first public schools were instituted in many southern states.[3]

Farmers, both Black and White, formed alliances. In 1886, 100,000 farmers had joined 2,000 alliance chapters. Black farmers organized the Colored Farmers' Alliance. They had a common cause to promote cooperative stores and manufacturers. While having a hand in whatever "concerned them as citizens". They would grow to as many as 400,000 members nationwide by 1889. Because they could not get the political reforms they desired, the alliance formed the "People's Party" in 1890.[3]

The People's Party (or Populist Party) had brought Blacks and Whites together like never before. In North Carolina, Black people were elected to office on the People's Party's ticket with White support. 24 Black delegates attended the People's Party's Convention in Georgia where party leader Tom Watson called for interracial unity. Black people who were voting in the South were still loyal to Republicans, but the People's Party was doing their best to pull them away.[3]

Then the southern Whites went crazy. This White ruling class had enough. The Klan started to come out in full force to wage assaults on interracial gatherings. Bourbon Democrats joined in on the witch hunt. Democrats still ran the courthouses and controlled most of the state legislatures throughout the South. The Democrats began to tighten their grip in the South adopting new state constitutions and passing laws to discourage both Black and poor White voters. Interracial gatherings became almost impossible. The poll tax and literacy test were put into place to further discourage voting. Laws were passed that made segregation mandatory. The races were to be separated. The alliance was over. Democrats made sure of it. In Washington D.C., things were just as messy during the postwar error as they were in the south. After the assassination of President Lincoln, Andrew Johnson sought to carry out the lenient reconstruction that Lincoln hoped to implement. This lenient reconstruction was stopped in its tracks before it could get started. The South had no intention of cooperating with a program that would force them to share power with Black people.[3]

Radical Republicans in the North, led by Thaddeus Stevens in the House of Representatives and Charles Sumner in the Senate, were determined to chastise the South and in the process make sure that the southern democratic power base would be unable to mount any type of resurgence. Democrats had managed to dominate national affairs up until that point, and Republicans had no appetite for a repeat.[2]

The southern states decided to enact "Black Codes" restricting the rights of former slaves on pretty much everything you could think of. Radical Republicans in Congress fired back by passing the Civil Rights Act of 1866 to protect Black people in the south. This protection would be incorporated in the 14th Amendment. President Andrew Johnson tried to stop Republicans in Congress from imposing such a radical brand of reconstruction. He exercised 29 vetoes only to see 15 of them over-ridden.[2]

Republicans enacted a number of laws at that time aimed at helping Black people. Besides the Civil Rights Act of 1866 that helped provide education, medical services and jobs to thousands of Black people in the South. Andrew Johnson finished out Lincoln's term and would never be seen anywhere near the White House again[2].

Ulysses Grant (a Republican) would cruise to victory. He favored the radical reconstruction as opposed to the more lenient bullshit favored by Andrew Johnson. Grant had been empowered by a number of so called force bills (from 1870-1871). He threatened the use of armed force against any state denying Black people the right to vote. His main target became the Ku Klux Klan. The Klan did their best to intimidate Black people into submission. They were particularly active in South Carolina. Grant decided to suspend Habeas Corpus and authorize mass arrest. Grant would also sign the Civil Rights Act of 1875 into law only to see the U.S. Supreme Court declare it unconstitutional in 1883.[2]

Rutherford Hayes, a cowardly Republican who wasn't even supposed to win the election, would withdraw federal troops from the South in 1877 as part of a compromise for allowing him to win a fraudulent election. The withdrawal of federal troops marked the end of reconstruction and it would be only a matter of time before Jim Crow would be in full force.[2]

The issue of race was still front and center in the U.S. in his inaugural address on March 4, 1881, Republican President James Garfield said: "The elevation of the Negro race from slavery to the full rights of citizenship is the most important political change we have known since the adoption of the Constitution in 1787."[2]

After Garfield's assassination, Chester Arthur would finish his term out. Then a Democrat would finally win the White House back, and coincidentally the issue of slavery or equality gets pushed to the backburner. Who would blame Grover Cleveland? That whole state rights fiasco will only take you so far when you are committing atrocities against a whole race of people.

Then as we take a very close look, we catch a glimpse of something very significant by historical proportions. In 1892, a guy by the name of James B. Weaver runs for president as a third party candidate on the People's (Populist) Party ticket.

Weaver was a native of Dayton, Ohio. He became a lawyer and ended up residing in Bloomfield, Iowa. He served in the Civil War and was a district attorney for a while. He abandoned the Republican Party and joined the Greenback Party. While in the Greenback Party he served in the U.S. House of Representatives on separate occasions. The Greenback Party evolved into the People's Party or the Populist Party. The Populist Platform was extremely liberal. The platform called for the nationalization of the railroads, telephone and telegraph. It called for a graduated income tax and the creation for postal savings banks. After losing the election to Grover Cleveland, Weaver led the Populist movement straight into the Democratic Party to throw support behind William Jennings Bryan. This seems to be the first real peak of liberal roots getting ready to be planted inside the Democratic Party. Up until this point, to be a liberal was to be a Republican.[2]

In the 1896 elections, William J. Bryan of Nebraska was the democratic nominee. The currency issue was the topic that dominated debate. Democrats were calling for free silver. The Republican platform supported the gold standard. This debate started to blur party lines. Silver Republicans in the West left the party to support Bryan. The Populist Party found itself in a strange position watching Democrats co-opt virtually every issue they had.

Democrats had finally seemed to catch on.[2]

After being confined to a regional party since the Civil War and realizing that they were getting pummeled by Republicans left and right, they started to become more flexible. This is our first real glimpse of liberalism taking shape in the Democratic Party. Eastern Democrats began to break ranks with the party because of the currency issue. They didn't want to support McKinley because of his tariff views, so they went and nominated their own candidate, John M. Palmer of Illinois. They called themselves the National or Gold Democrats.[2]

Mayor Tom Johnson of Cleveland summed up the campaign as, "The first great protest of the American people against monopoly—the first great struggle of the masses in our country against privileged classes." Bryan was looked at as a radical socialist. McKinley was accused of being a puppet for the capitalist.[2]

Just because Democrats were starting to get liberal doesn't mean Republicans were suddenly becoming conservative. The McKinley Administration was for the gains in women's rights and pledged "equal pay for equal work". In 1900, McKinley called for such things as raising the age limit for child labor and condemned southern laws that kept Black people from the polls.

In 1904, Democrats nominated a conservative Democrat by the name of Alton Parker to run against Theodore Roosevelt. William J. Bryan decided not to run again so they settled on Parker who got whipped by Roosevelt in the election. After the thorough thumping at the hands of Roosevelt, Democrats had no stomach for another Alton Parker. It was the time to bring William J. Bryan back. This was the turning point for Democrats. Progressives under Bryan now owned the party and his supporters rocked the party's National Convention in June of 1908.[2] They were dominate throughout the convention and the shift in the party was visible.

In his inaugural address, William Taft mentions the strides Black people have made and hope for even more progress. He talked about this being "their" country as well. He concludes that it is a "sacred duty" to make the path of Black people "smooth and easy". It's also important to note that under Taft the Constitution was ratified under the 16th Amendment. The Congress now had the power to lay and collect taxes on incomes. This little piece of information is relevant because when Taft would go up for re-election Teddy Roosevelt would pop up from nowhere and challenge him for the Republican nomination. Roosevelt did this on the grounds that Republicans were becoming too conservative.

Well, Democrats didn't seem to be having that problem. The party was deeply divided as to who the nominee should be.

William J. Bryan was not going to run again but he was the titular head of the party. His influence was huge and progressives would follow his lead. He would end up endorsing Woodrow Wilson.[2]

Meanwhile, Theodore Roosevelt was on the verge of hurting the Republican Party. You see, he didn't actually do two whole terms in the White House. He was vice president when William McKinley was assassinated. He finished out McKinley's term and cruised to victory in the next election. He said to run for president again would feel too much like a third term, so he stepped aside and endorsed his own good friend, William H. Taft. Roosevelt left as a hero to Republicans.

He was a popular, charismatic president who used his bully pulpit to get a lot done. He had two whirlwind terms that left the country breathless and hoping for more. His good friend William Taft was grateful for the endorsement, and was prepared to carry out the Roosevelt agenda.

Then in 1912, Roosevelt pops up from nowhere and decides he wants the Republican nomination. Confused and bewildered Republicans who looked up to Roosevelt, had to tell him to go sit his silly ass down somewhere. Taft was the guy. It made no sense to just abandon him now. Instead of having some type of rational understanding, Roosevelt decided to run on a third party ticket. He became the "Bull Moose" candidate or what should been known as the "Bullshit" candidate.

Roosevelt ran as a progressive, and the liberals in the party decided to follow him. This caused a major split inside the party and it divided the Republican vote. Thus the election tilted toward Woodrow Wilson. Wilson, thanks to the chaos inside the Republican party, would enjoy two terms as president.

While in office, Wilson carried out a pretty liberal

agenda, passing such laws as the Federal Reserve Act of 1913 and the Keating Owen Act of 1916 (which ended up being struck down by the Supreme Court in Hammer v. Dagenhart, 1918). This led Congress to pass the Child Labor Act of 1919. This law placed a ten percent tax on the profits of companies employing children. The Constitution was ratified in 1913. One of the amendments to be ratified was the 19th Amendment which gave women the right to vote.[2]

In the election of 1920, Democrats nominated the liberal James Cox. Cox was a successful governor of Ohio and served in the U.S. House. He would lose to the moderate Republican, Warren Harding. The major issue that separated the candidates was concerning the League of Nations which was established during the Wilson era.[2]

Warren G. Hardin would become the first president since the Civil War to go into the South and in a southern state to speak out on behalf of Black people. This took place on October 26, 1921 in Birmingham, Alabama. Inside the university that's home to the Crimson Tide, Harding lectured a segregated audience on the importance of racial equality.[2] Democrats might have given women the right to vote but Republicans were still the party dedicated to Black people. After Harding's unexpected death in office, Calvin Coolidge would finish out his term. His huge tax breaks for the rich in 1924 and 1926 might have been a sign of things to come, but Republicans were still pretty normal for the most part. Then the train wreck known as Herbert Hoover would come crashing into town. After the Stock Market Crash of 1929, Hoover acted like he was living in some parallel universe detached from the reality that the economy had just tanked. In March of 1930, Hoover would declare, "All the evidences indicate that the worst effects of the crash upon unemployment will have passed during the next 60 days." While Hoover was clearly living in some happy place deep down in some hidden corridor in the back of his brain, unemployment was skyrocketing. This wasn't just a gaffe. He reiterated this same bunch of crap a few months later. Hoover would become a symbol of the crisis. While he was trying trickle-down economics, giving a helping hand to people who didn't need the money, the homeless were calling their collection of cardboard houses "Hooverville". Keep in mind many of these people were middle class and poor Whites along with Black people.

In May of 1932, over 15,000 veterans marched on Washington to demand immediate payment of bonuses that had been overdue since 1924. Hoover would order the bonus camp to be cleared out. General Douglas MacArthur, Major Dwight Eisenhower, and Major George Patton would lead four cavalry troops equipped with fixed bayonets along with tear gas and tanks against some veterans and their families. One infant was killed from the tear gas and a small boy was stabbed in the leg while trying to save his pet rabbit. After destroying the "enemy", the cavalry set fire to their shacks.[2]

This use of armed force to defeat a bunch of unarmed families only re-enforced the perception that Hoover was a heartless piece of shit. I, personally believe that perception gives him way too much credit. Coward and scumbag have to be in the description to at least start the conversation. Herbert Hoover is one of the worst things to ever happen to Republicans. Teddy Roosevelt might have divided the party and probably (inadvertently) drove progressives into the arms of Democrats, but Herbert Hoover created a true identity crisis for Republicans. It is amazing how one man could screw a whole party, humiliate himself so badly, and hurt so many Americans with his sheer incompetence. A real trifecta.

Hoover was ushered out of office like one of those people on Apollo Theater when the "Sandman" comes unto the stage and dances their goofy asses back behind the curtains. Hoover's welcomed departure would open the door to a "New Deal".

Franklin Delano Roosevelt (F.D.R.) would destroy Hoover in the election and transform the role of government along with the political landscape. F.D.R. launched the New Deal his first year in office (1933). The New Deal was a huge unprecedented program that provided federal relief, economic regulation, and established today's social safety net. Social Security along with other laws that came from the New Deal had a positive effect on the poor.[2]

Many of these poor people were Black. The New Deal produced a backlash from Republicans that allowed many of the conservatives in the party to find their voice. Republicans felt the New Deal "dishonored American tradition" and wanted the federal program to be turned over to the states. The voters on the other hand didn't want to hear it. Roosevelt won re-election carrying all but two states in a landslide victory.

While campaigning for re-election, Roosevelt received

endorsements from the National Association for the Advancement of Colored People. That sealed the deal. This was the decisive shift that had been brewing. The Black vote had officially abandoned the Party of Lincoln and became loyal to the Democrats. Roosevelt and congressional Democrats implemented programs through the New Deal that were having a positive impact. Black people finally saw something more than lip service while the rich got tax breaks. Republicans wanted to see the New Deal done away with and this gave many middle class and poor people flashbacks to Hoover. Republicans became the foil F.D.R. needed whenever he wanted to get something done. Democrats were now the compassionate "can do" party. Republicans seemed grumpy and out of touch.[2]

F.D.R. died a few months into his fourth term. His Vice President, Harry Truman would take his place. Truman would sign into law the Housing Act of 1949. Also known as the "Fair Deal". It sent federal funds for slum clearance and federal renewal, it increased minimum wage, extended Social Security and desegregated the military. The desegregation of the military was huge. It laid the groundwork for the march towards civil rights which was only a few years away from catching fire.[2] This reinforced the view by Black people that Democrats were the only ones trying to help them in their plight. Conservatives grumbled about the Fair Deal, especially the desegregation of the armed forces.

As mentioned earlier, Eisenhower was not the ideologue Hoover was and in no way resembled his stupidity. Because of this, Eisenhower managed to woo back some of the Black vote to Republicans. During the

1956 campaign, he repeatedly point out his efforts to enforce desegregation in schools. The GOP launched a task force in 1956 to campaign in Black neighborhoods and Adam Clayton Powell, a Democrat from New York, endorsed Eisenhower. Powell was extremely popular in the Black community. These efforts helped Eisenhower receive 40 percent of the Black vote.[2] No Republican nominee has come close to receiving that type of support from Black people since.

Richard Nixon added civil rights to the Republican platform only because of a deal he made with Governor Nelson Rockefeller of New York on the eve of the convention. Rockefeller agreed not only to step aside, but to also endorse Nixon for the Republican nomination. The bright lines, however, would be drawn in the sand concerning race.

In October of 1960, the Rev. Dr. Martin Luther King Jr. was arrested in Atlanta during a sit in demonstration. Kennedy decided to personally call Mrs. King to offer his assistance. This was taking place while Robert F. Kennedy was contacting a local judge to arrange for King's bail. Not long after that Dr. King's father issued a statement saying that his original intent was to vote for Nixon, but he decided to switch because: "Jack Kennedy has the moral courage to stand up for what he knows is right." Kennedy ran away with the Black vote. To Black people it seemed Nixon was all about lip service but Kennedy showed action.[2] Just like that, the small strides Eisenhower made in pulling Black people back to the GOP were gone for good. Liberals took action, it was that simple.

The Civil Rights Movement was hitting a fever pitch in the early 60's. Kennedy responded to the movement with executive action. In November of 1962, he ordered an end to discrimination in housing owned, operated, or financed by the federal government. He then established the president's committee on Equal Employment Opportunity. He appointed numerous Black people to high ranking federal positions. In June of 1963, he gave a moving address to a live television audience challenging Americans to live up to the ideals of freedom.[2]

After the tragic assassination of President Kennedy, Lyndon Johnson would finish his term out. It didn't take long for Johnson to implement the war on poverty and sign into law the Civil Rights of 1964. This was the government intervention that was needed.

Republicans nominated Barry "The Circus Clown" Goldwater to be the sacrificial idiot to be beat up on by Lyndon B. Johnson. Goldwater was an opponent of the civil rights bills. His position on civil rights garnered just three percent support from Black people.

Three percent might seem really low, but I am trying to figure out what those three percent of Black people were thinking when they supported Goldwater. I mean, let's be serious, do Herman Cain and Clarence Thomas have that many connections or did those two jerkoffs tamper with the ballots? I see a conspiracy theory taking shape.

By the time Republicans got the White House back their image was unshakable. Even though Nixon governed from the center and pretty much played it safe on race and civil rights issues Black people remained loyal to Democrats.

Black people got behind Jimmy Carter even though he made some gaffes during the election that made some wonder if he was really an undercover racist. Despite carrying 90 percent of the Black vote, Carter was pummeled by Reagan.

Ronald Reagan not only reinforced Black people's perception of the GOP, he confirmed it. Blacks in poverty were still waiting for the money to trickle down from the Reagan tax cuts and the only programs Reagan cut in his budgets were those that benefited the poor.

In the 90's it was Republicans who shut the government down because Clinton refused cuts in Medicare. Welfare reform was even rejected twice by Clinton because congressional Republicans were too radical with the cuts. Once again, Republicans showed complete disregard for those who needed help most.

Hurricane Katrina ripped the city of New Orleans apart in August of 2005. The lackadaisical response by the Bush Administration smacked of racism. It might seem like an unfair verdict, but many people around the country were outraged to see a White president playing a guitar in California—and having a blast at that—while a thousand Black people stood on rooftops, surrounded by water, screaming and pleading for help. This was probably just an act of an incompetent, callous, irresponsible administration. Nevertheless, perception can be reality, and that was the perception that was projected. Like it or not.

Then, of course, there was the ultimate slap in the face to Black people. In the summer of 2010, Steve Kohlhagen, a former professor at Cal-Berkley was the star witness before the Financial Crisis Inquiry Commission. He was testifying as to what caused the financial crisis. He felt that over the counter derivatives and certain credit default swaps had "absolutely no role whatsoever in causing the financial crisis". This, of course, was a bunch of horseshit. Mortgage backed CDO's caused Wachovia to go belly up and certain types of credit default swaps is what destroyed AIG.[1]

He goes on to say, "The cause of the financial crisis was quite simply the commitment by the United States Government to bring homeownership to the next group of people who previously had not been able to own their own homes."

Translation:
This crisis wasn't caused by greedy, selfish, irresponsible, dickhead bankers who lead giant behemoth sized institutions that made shitloads of money and then took that money along with money that didn't really belong to them and gamble it away faster than Michael Jordan at a golf tournament because they knew the government would save their scumbag asses. No, what screwed the economy was poor Black people who were forced by their own government into buying houses that they knew damn well they couldn't afford.[1]

Now you really have to understand the setting to appreciate such an audacious lie. This guy, Kohlhagen, once was the head of the derivatives and risk management desk at First Union. First Union was the predecessor to

Wachovia, which was a huge megabank. In fact, it was one of the largest banks in the country. Because of its lousy mortgage backed derivatives it was forced to merger with Wells Fargo in October of 2008. At first, Wells Fargo rejected the proposition of rescuing Wachovia, but Treasury Secretary and Wall St. tramp, Hank Paulson made them an offer they couldn't refuse. First, he rigged the tax code so that Wells Fargo was promised a 25 billion dollar tax break. Then Bush signed TARP into law which gave Wells Fargo another 25 billion.[1]

On October 3, a day after the bailout was passed, Wells Fargo had a sudden injection and compassion and decided to lend the government a helping hand. They bought Wachovia for 12.7 billion dollars. Thanks to the bailout (paid for by taxpayers) Wells Fargo was able to dish out 977 million dollars in bonuses. Now that's how you celebrate on taxpayer money.[1]

Steven Kohlhagen is one of the reasons Wachovia no longer exists. He helped stack the bank's books with toxic mortgage backed CDO's. Now he's at a FCIC hearing blaming the crisis on poor people. After he testified, another jerkoff by the name of Albert Kyle, a professor of finance at Maryland University, would testify that "government mandates for homeownership was the main reason for the crisis." I guess I don't need to keep translating these idiots.[1]

Republicans picked up on this convenient little narrative. They began complaining about the Community Reinvestment Act of 1977, and then it was Fannie and Freddie.[1]

A Republican senator from Alabama named Richard Shelby gave one of the best quotes: "Private enterprise mixed with social engineering" is what led to the collapse. This is the Republicans way of saying that the government tried too hard to look out for all those lazy black people, who in return made us all pay for such compassionate stupidity.[1]

It's no secret that the Community Reinvestment Act of 1977 was a law targeted to guard against discrimination in the housing market. To say it led to the housing collapse thirty years later is not only ridiculous, it gives you an idea about the conservative mindset. A law is passed that might benefit minorities, and conservatives hate it and then come with a bunch of fairy tales to make that law responsible for the calamity. This, I suppose, is to justify their logic behind such distaste for the law or laws in question. Yet, rich people who worked for mega institutions are actually the one's responsible for the worst economic shake up in eight decades and they form a queue, lavish them with praise, and then use a false verisimilitude to defend their warped ideology. Anyone who dares question such imperceptible wisdom is nothing more than an envious, impecunious peasant trying to wage class warfare against the best and the brightest. You really have to admire the nerve of these people.

So, you catch a glimpse of the pattern here? Conservatives have not only never been interested in using government on behalf of those who need it, but they have pretty much opposed it. To make matters worse conservatives use a disguised language to state how they really feel. They want to shrink the safety net for the poor to empower them with jobs. Instead of giving Black people food stamps they would rather give them a paycheck for an honest day's work.

It is a known fact that some people will try to play games with the system, but here's a stunning revelation: most poor people don't like being poor. Hello!! The vast majority of Americans would like to have a job and would prefer making 100,000 dollars a year instead of living off of 5,000 dollars a year in government subsidies.

Yes, there are a few out there who don't mind living off of food stamps. But dare I say, 95 percent of Americans who live in poverty would much rather have a stable job than government assistance. Only an idiot who has never been poor could say such misinformed bullshit. Only a bigot who's detached from the suffering of others could justify that crap with some "can do" rhetoric.

Conservatives don't really believe their own rhetoric, it's just that by framing such a quixotic argument that they have some type of justification for exercising their own rigid ideology. As I said before, Republicans are 97 percent White and the Tea Party is about 99 percent White. They have a history of being insensitive toward minorities, especially Black people which abandoned the party because of their lackadaisical approach to their needs and concerns. However, it's not their driving motive against the president. It probably adds a lot of fuel to their fire, but it's clear there is a bigger player at hand. Conservatives might be just as wacko right now if Hillary Clinton was president. Remember, they shut the government down on Bill Clinton. Maybe it could be looked at as a double motive. There is no doubt that a Black president with a Muslim name has completely shaken their world view.

But as shown in the last chapter, conservatives have a pattern of going wacko when their party is not in power. This is another one of those times that the sore losers try to regain their grip. Race is not the main motivation. Conservatives (not all but most) were racist long before the president ever walked into the White House.

Another perspective that needs to be mentioned is the Herman Cain high. The Tea Party loves Herman Cain *despite* the fact he's Black. At least I am pretty sure he's Black. Judging from the evidence we're pretty sure he's Black. Anyway, even though conservatives have shown an inability to connect with Black people, winning back power is way more important. A Black conservative in the White House is better than no conservative at all.

Tea Party members were ecstatic to see a Black person so passionately believe the same bullshit they did. Cain was their validation on social issues and would help them be seen in a different light. "Ya see", they probably said amongst themselves, "if all negroes were like the Cain boy, we would like them too."

Unfortunately for conservatives, the Herminator, as he was affectionately called, might have been Black on the outside but he was a White woman's worst nightmare on the inside.

So as mentioned before, racism might add a certain element of hysteria to the current conservative movement, but the power grab is the ultimate goal.

So, is there another option? If it's not racism, then what else? The next option to explore is one of mental capacity. Maybe the Tea Party are the most stupid people to ever walk the Earth. There is some viable evidence to support this option as well.

First, the Tea Party rallied around a call to arms by a PR whore for Wall Street. Then they protested Obama's stimulus despite the fact the polls showed they had no idea what was in the package or what the money was being spent on. They didn't even know that 40 percent of the stimulus was a bunch of tax breaks, something they cry out for every chance they get. The Tea Party blossomed when they started protesting the law even though polls show they still have no idea what was (or is) in it.

Many in the Tea Party thought the president was a Muslim and that he was born in another country. In one survey, 25 percent of them thought he was the Antichrist.

The Tea Party opposes the big government agenda of Obama but supported the big government agenda of George W. Bush when they re-elected him. Of course, they didn't have a clue as to what Bush was doing, right?

Maybe it's because the Tea Party gets all their information from Fox News. Fox endorsed Bush, so "they" endorsed Bush. Fox discredits the current president so "they" discredit the current president. A side note: one poll showed people that watch Fox News actually become 12 percent dumber every year.

So, maybe these good old freedom fighters are just a bunch of well-intentioned dummies who want their guns back and the government out of their back yard. Well, let's face it, they might be misinformed, but they are not stupid. They know exactly what they are doing and why they're doing it.

They claim they want Reagan back, but Reagan did much of the things they protest against right now. Maybe they really are stupid when it comes to Reagan, but I think they know better. At some point they found this stuff out.

Another sign the Tea Party might be just that stupid occurred right before the 2010 mid-term elections. The Tea Party forced the GOP to sign pledges, take oaths, sign contracts, spank each other, etc. The GOP candidates fell all over themselves trying to convince the Tea Party they were not just conservative, but they were super-duper, ultra, beyond reality conservative.

Anyway, the 2010 mid-term elections were about to get underway and it was clear that the GOP were on the verge of taking control of the House. This feat was in large part due to the Tea Party. They had controlled the narrative and their influence was being felt nationwide.

John Boehner knew that if Republicans took control of the House that he would probably be speaker. Unless, of course, the Tea Party didn't want him to be. You see, what the Tea Party wants, the Tea Party gets. Boehner had reason to wonder if the Tea Party was really hip on him. He had a lengthy track record of voting for things that were not paid for. Not to mention his love for big tobacco and big banks. His most expensive unpaid vote was TARP. The 700 billion dollar bailout program.

What Boehner didn't realize is that the Tea Party didn't give a shit who the Speaker of the House was. As long as it wasn't Nancy Pelosi, they were satisfied. The Tea Party wanted Republicans in power, that's it. Boehner's track record clearly didn't bother them. He did all that stuff when a Republican was president. Since the Democrat has been in there he's been a faithful obstructionist.

Well, Boehner either didn't realize this or he just wanted to make it look like he was the face of the party. Ya know, get his name in a few national headlines. Maybe he thought he could draw as much attention as Newt Gingrich did back in the 90's when he was Speaker of the House.

So Boehner decided to really flex his stupidity. First he feels the need to win the party over, they of course didn't care if Barney Fife was the next speaker. So, to win them over he tells a bold faced lie that would be exposed only a few short months after the election.

He goes and steals the spotlight by vowing to cut 100 billion dollars in discretionary spending out of the budget. This leads to the second reason why Boehner lacks the brains of a cockroach who inhaled too much Raid. The Tea Party seems to know nothing about economics. All they know is that the government is spending trillions of dollars and that the deficit is over a trillion. They know that for sure, they probably investigated it on Fox News.
So, 100 billion dollars not only sounded believable but it

seemed like a drop in the bucket. This did very little to excite the base. Instead it seemed to disappoint them a great deal. There was a lot of grumbling that the new regime was promising too little. After some prodding, the movement begrudgingly was learning to live with the whole 100 billion dollar promise.

So, Boehner opened his mouth with a pointless lie and did little to convince them that he is a born again conservative. Instead it somewhat deflated them. The Tea Party matched his stupidity by believing him. A few months after the mid-term election, the climatic budget battle took place. It wasn't all that climatic though. In fact, it was a bunch of grandstanding and the same old predictable bullshit. Re-runs of Happy Days and the Jeffersons garnered higher ratings than the CNN's intense coverage of the so-called budget battle. The Tea Party protested on the steps of the Capitol demanding that the government be shut down if they couldn't get their way. "No Compromise" was the mantra. At the 11th hour of the fight, Republicans got just what they didn't want. They got a compromise for only 38 billion in cuts. They were 62 billion short of their 100 billion dollar promise. The Tea Party couldn't believe this shit.

To make matters worse, the CBO exposed that the cuts weren't real. According to the CBO, only 352 *million* was cut, which means Republicans actually fell 99 billion short of their 100 billion dollar promise. The rest was a sorry ass spending gimmick.

The Tea Party actually bought into the lie without even questioning where the cuts would come from or how they planned to ram it through a Democratic-controlled Senate. They also didn't bother to ask what the alternative would be if they couldn't push the 100 billion dollar promise through Congress. Instead they heard a number, got their pledges and swooped Republicans into power. It's so easy to dupe the Tea Party.

Even now, the Tea Party has quietly grumbled about the fact that some of the clowns they ushered into office were not keeping their promises. Of course, they're going to re-elect them.

So, what's the verdict? Have I misjudged the Tea Party? Are they really not after power, but instead are just a bunch of idiots who don't have a clue as to what's being said or done until after it happens. The answer is no.

Yes, the Tea Party is misinformed and clueless about a great many things. It's not because their stupid though. It's because their minds are made up. They are a bunch of narrow-minded ideologues who are lifelong Republicans. They are committed to regaining the upper hand. Other information is irrelevant because it interferes with their agenda. The left is wrong no matter what and Republicans are right no matter what. Here's some proof...

Despite the fact that John Boehner lied to them with a straight face on several occasions (concerning the 100 billion dollar promise) the Tea Party will support him in November 2012. Boehner might be a lying sack of horseshit who sheds fake crocodile tears to get some positive press coverage, but guess what? He's their lying sack of horseshit. He's with the home team. He's a

Republican, so his logic is understood.

The Tea Party organized like a well-oiled machine during the 2010 mid-term elections. They are far from stupid. The information is irrelevant. If a Republican says tax cuts for the rich stimulate the economy it must be true. To hell with sound economics. All science is a bunch of mumbo jumbo bullshit that elitist want you to believe. Facts are not really facts if the source that it's coming from at that moment might have liberal tendencies.

Many at the bottom of the movement might feel they have good intentions. All they want is their country back — whatever the hell that means — but for them to be led astray by the upper echelon of the party is a testament to their own ideology, world view, and loyalties. It's a testament to what type of America they envision.

It's an America where rich people are to be worshipped no matter how much criminal damage they do to the economy. They are to be catered to even at the cost of the poor. It's an America where Black people deserve the injustices they receive because they are simply trying to push their way into government assistance and turn our beautiful free market into a welfare state.

It's an America where Hispanics *look* suspicious so they should be harassed if they want the privilege of living in our great country. It's an America where women stay at home, make babies, and shut the hell up. It's an America where gay people can be accepted as long as they acknowledge that they are the purest form of scum to ever walk the Earth and do so by keeping their sexual preferences a deep dark secret. It's an America where good person means Christian and everybody else is just a bunch of terrorists trying to declare war on the <u>true</u> religion.

It's an America where war supporters (without question) are patriots, anything less is treason. It's an America that says you're only poor because you're lazy. To be deceived by a mortgage company or become collateral damage by the greed of Wall St. makes you incompetent and irresponsible.

That's the America conservatives want back. It's one that they will never have back, because this generation will not allow that type of regression. The Republicans have a long history of promoting this type of America. It's the type of America that eases their own insecurities. It's one that makes them the centerpiece of the country. It rationalizes their stereotype and confirms their quixotic ideal concerning right and wrong. It gives them the power, it promotes their agenda and reminds them of a time when only simple solutions for simple problems existed.

If there is still cause to doubt my theory about the Tea Party's motives I have saved the best and most obvious example for last. Just take a look at the Republican primaries of 2011-12. Republicans have fallen in love with almost every candidate in the race at some point yet they are embracing Mitt Romney. A Massachusetts "moderate". Moderate is putting it gently.

The Tea Party has openly admitted that they don't like Mitt Romney, but if it means beating Barack Obama they will rally to his side. Even though the Tea Party favors

Rick Santorum (as of this writing) they admit that Santorum can't win. So they're going with Romney for the sole purpose of winning.

It's the same calculations that motivated them to get behind Bush and every other candidate that they've supported over the last several decades. Despite the fact that Romney has been for everything before he was against it. In fact, he could have run as a Democrat. The man has agreed with everything that means something to someone at some point. For the Tea Party, it doesn't matter. It's all about a Republican, even one that passed a healthcare bill while he was the Governor of Massachusetts that strongly resembles Obamacare. It's a bill that he once said could work on a national level.

If the Tea Party wanted to show that they were true lovers of the Constitution who would not accept just any old RINO (Republican In Name Only), they would sit out the presidential election as protest. Or they would get a third party candidate just to show Republicans that without their support they will be derailed so they better respect their dissatisfaction with the current front runner. But they won't.

Because the Tea Party is not a third party. They are Republicans, and if Romney gives them their best chance to win they will go through hell and high water to get to the polls and vote for him. They will get behind the moderate (converted conservative). And if he wins, being moderate will be cool again. Unless he wins as a conservative. These people have acted radical as a tactic to win back the White House.

If that tactic isn't going to work, they will change tactics. It's about beating Obama and reclaiming the White House. The Tea Party would rather rally around some jackass from a reality show if they thought he gave them their best shot to beat Obama. No offense Donald Trump. They actually did flock to Trump until polls showed he would be dismantled by Obama in a one on one race.

There it is, the facts in a nutshell. The Tea Party is the Republican Party. Their agenda is not a balanced budget or the Constitution. Their agenda is Party. They are Republicans. Their gripe is not about a bill, it's politics. They have been playing political games for the last three years. They want their country back and apparently the only way to get it back is to first take the White House. It's all about a selfish **Power Grab**.

4 | VOODOO ECONOMICS: TAX CUTS FOR THE RICH NEVER WORK

So many Americans have been wounded by the policies of Washington. America is multifarious, but no matter what the race, religion or gender the economic crisis has been felt by all of the middle class and poor. From Salt Lake to Bloomington. From San Jose to Daytona.

Just ask the farmer in the Midwest, to the salesman on the East Coast. Or how about the fisherman in Louisiana and the small business owner in Nevada. Look at the fear in the eyes of a senior citizen living day to day on a pension or listen to the frustration in the voice of a 25 year old trying to pay back a college loan that often cuts into his or her rent money.

These are the people who represent the statistics in the unemployment rate, under employment, and the poverty rate. These are the type of people who watched the rich get showered with tax cuts during the Bush era while they struggled to make ends meet. They are the people who lost their homes, and the many that went on to lose their jobs when the rug came from under the economy in 2008. They are the people who saw their wages go flat over the last thirty years while the richest one percent saw a whopping 250 percent increase.

Whenever these facts are brought to light, conservatives prattle about "class warfare". It's class warfare whenever you state facts about the middle class getting screwed, but it's a theatrical sympathy fest when Goldman Sachs is accused of being run by crooked thieves. The rich are to be seen as the standard of American excellence. Luminaries allowing the rest of us to worship their bold vision. We should also ossify to this superior logic so that we can add some type of purpose to our own feeble quotidian existence. Anything less would simply vitiate the accomplishments of such chosen ones. To commit such transgressions against America's finest would be the act of a quisling. How dare anyone disrepute such talent! Liberal peasants are trying to surreptitiously punish the noble visionaries, for they are envious and jealous...yeah right!!!

The fact is most normal people who are middle class and poor (almost the same thing) have nothing against the rich. I applaud them. I don't think rich people should be punished for being rich. I just don't think poor people should have to be suffer for the fuck ups of the rich. I hope I become rich, and I hope many others who are struggling become rich as well. Hell, I hope the rich get richer.

This is one of the many reasons America is the greatest

country on the planet. We have the right to become rich. We have the right to innovate and create. We have the right to unleash our potential and shoot for the stars. To feel any type of animosity toward the rich would be a sick, twisted, immature, perverse logic.

What I, and many others, resent is the fact that the rich people who caused this economic meltdown are rewarded with bailouts (bought and paid for with taxpayer money) then they high five each other and celebrate with giving themselves huge bonuses. Meanwhile, the middle class and poor are treated like a bunch of faceless numbers who burden the budget. Unemployment benefits cost too much and besides they are an incentive not to work. A middle class tax cut should expire because it's not a proven job creator. Yet they fight tooth and nail to make the Bush tax cuts (for the wealthy) permanent. When did they become proven job creators? Is this not obvious?

Class warfare is taking place, but it's being fought on behalf of the rich, not the poor. They preach against a divisive politics, but turn around and rig the tax code with a multitude of loop holes for millionaires.

After this goodie bag of treats becomes too expensive they cut programs for the poor to pay for them. This is not capitalism. It's a warped perverse form of socialism. Instead of taking from the rich to give to the poor, they take from the poor and give to the rich. They want to reduce the size of government in the middle class—Medicare and Social Security—but use the government to swoop in and save the rich—TARP. They use your tax dollars for a bailout and then tell you that your tax dollars are not enough for <u>your</u> bailout—unemployment benefits. Government intervention for the middle class is socialism. You have got to be shitting me!!!

Conservatives in our government want to turn Medicare into a voucher program to finance a tax cut for Bill Gates. That's not an exaggeration either. All House conservatives voted for Paul "Asshole" Ryan's budget last year, and this year all but ten in the House have. All Senate Republicans except five voted for it. The budgets have also been embraced by every GOP Presidential candidate.

These people have the audacity to basically look at Main Street and say: "We, the government, now have to kick you in your ass. You see, after spending all your money on the same people who caused you to be unemployed and almost homeless we're broke." So they come with a courageous budget that features "steep cuts"…on the victim!

It's absurd. Nobody is mad with Lebron James, Garth Brooks, Jay-Z, Denzel Washington, Harrison Ford or Mel Gibson…well, maybe Mel's ex-wife…and probably Jewish people, a lot of Black people and anybody who's ever had to work with him, but I digress. Sorry. Nobody has ever complained about these folks being rich—with the exception of Mel maybe—or protested Hollywood for paying Brad Pitt 20 million dollars to star in a movie. If anything, this is the type of information that inspires people to become actors. Nobody is protesting outside of the Staple Center because Kobe Bryant got a 140 million dollar contract extension. Laker fans are happy. Celtic fans hate him because he's a Laker and the rest of us are just worried about the cost of the beer and how long the line to the bathroom is gonna be for halftime.

This whole defensive accusation about punishing the rich is nothing more than a diversion from the real issue of justice. To surmise such a backward logic is ridiculous. To even ignore such legitimate anger and frustration is either a way to sidestep the facts or it's a symptom of mild retardation. This type of bullshit rhetoric is casuistic at best. This is like a judge in court telling a rape victim, "Congratulations ma'am, we caught the rapist. Now I am going to order you to *pay him* to sodomize you all over again. If you complain it's because you're just envious of the fact he has a pecker and you don't."

Conservatives are entrenched in this myth. Many of them have enough sense to know it's not true, but they spew it to their base anyway. This whole spoil the rich method has never stimulated an economic boom. It has, on the other hand, caused a serious contraction of the middle class. We have 50 million Americans living in poverty. 50 million! That's insane for a country that has an economy worth 15 trillion dollars. How many do you think were once considered "middle class"? The middle class has contracted so much over the last thirty years that it's hard to tell the difference between the two classes. The wealth gap has widened immensely over the last three decades, and it's only getting worse.

If this was just some unintended consequence of capitalism I could understand. If this phenomenon was the result of free enterprise taking it's natural course of action then I would have no complaints. But that's not the case at all. This has been the acts of some idiotic ideologues who frequently impose the same tried and failed policies over and over. With deliberate disregard to the collateral damage (the American people) they don't pull back. They double down. It's as if they feel that if they do this shit enough that somehow it will finally work. Then they can finally say I told you so. Vindication at last. Their economic ideology is not just flawed it's irrational. Americans may not all be economist, but we know when we're not getting a fair shake.

But this type of language is disregarded as "class warfare". How dare we state the facts! Government needs to shrink…except when it comes to bailouts and a bullshit tax code skewed in favor of the mega rich.

This perverse, detached, and amazingly retarded logic could not be justified if you melted it down into a great big ball of fire, and shoved it straight up the ass of Sean Hannity. After which, he throws up a giant nugget of gold.

In the first three chapters we have seen just how full of shit conservatives are. But nothing exemplifies their dangerousness to the country more than their economic views. It's one thing to want to derail the economy because there is a Democrat in the White House. It's a horse of a different color when a Republican is in the White House and they do it by accident. Their party is committed to an economic ideology that is nothing more than wishful thinking. Nothing is more intertwined, however, to the political aspect of this movement than the economic aspect. To truly understand the essence of any political organization, movement, etc…just check out the economic agenda. The fact that they have used every childish tactic under the sun is one thing. That might be reason enough to dislike them. It's what they might do *if* they regain power, that should worry people.

I could go into details on social issues that are of extreme importance. I could delve into the fact that conservatives want women to have about as many rights as a female convicted felon on house arrest...in Saudi Arabia! I could also go into the fact that many Black people are treated like unwanted in-laws who rudely just dropped in for Thanksgiving and wore out their welcome drinking up all the wine. All the while their dog keeps pissing on the welcome mat. We could even talk about how conservatives are biased toward religions that disagree with their own. Like the fact that all Muslims should be investigated for possible terrorism. Catholics are cool when they oppose abortion, but when they propose immigration reform it's because they are secret liberals trying to impose the will of the Pope. They feel like Mormons are a cult trying to kidnap young girls for breeding purposes as they hide them with their other 35 wives.

Yes, all these topics are relevant to so many people. But the one topic that ties them all together is economics. Economic policies affect me and you, no matter who you are. The easiest way to advance a political or social agenda is through economics. Politics is the driver of history, but economics is the driver of politics. Think about it. I can impose my social philosophy by cutting funding for Planned Parenthood. I feel poor people are just lazy, so I cut programs out of the budget that help the poor. Oil companies fund my campaign so I make sure they get a bunch of special tax breaks. I do this all in the name of economics. No need for numerous pieces of legislation. One budget, and I can reshape the social order of the country.

Through economics there is justice and injustice. When Dr. King marched and preached for civil rights he didn't just ask America to accept Black people. He asked for jobs. Social justice is achieved through economic justice. Money can lift a nation and a lack of money can destroy a nation. Equal pay for women when they do equal work is equality.

If you want to cripple a certain class of people just hinder their economic status. If I had two sons I could treat them equally by giving them both the same amount of money. Then I punish them by cutting their allowance for a month. This would be considered justice. Outside of incarceration the main way to institute a perceived form of justice is through money. And even the criminal justice system is skewed toward the wealthy. The rich have to come out of their pocketbook to stay out of prison. The poor go to prison for being poor on many occasions. This is justice in America. There are exceptions to every rule, but this is definitely the norm.

So, the economic aspect and the political aspect go hand in hand. Bill Clinton once said, "Politics is about economics. People forget that the New Deal was an economic program. A lot of social good came out of it, but it was an economic program."

That's exactly right. It was an economic program that changed the social landscape. Our economic philosophy has always been a reflection of who we are as a people.

The conservative economic ideology is a reflection of who they are and what they stand for. It's an ideology that says the economy is driven by the rich. So, they are to be pandered to at all cost. The rest of us are to sacrifice because if we don't tote the burdens of injustice the rich might suffer. If the rich suffer the Earth will tilt off its axis and hurl us all straight into the sun. The rich must get justice at all cost and then the rest of us can anxiously await for the justice to trickle on down.

"We cannot finance the country, we cannot improve social conditions, through any system of injustice, even if we attempt to inflict it on the rich. It is absurd to suppose that it is envious of those who are already prosperous." Calvin Coolidge spoke those words at his inaugural address on March 4, 1925. He would go on and cut taxes, in 1924 and 1926, for the wealthy. The economy did pretty well while Coolidge was in office. Many conservatives took this as the tax cuts for the rich were the reason. Maybe so. The economy was already starting a boom cycle when he cut taxes, but that could be debatable.

I myself, don't think the tax cuts did anything, but I could be wrong. I base my opinion on a few things. Herbert Hoover used the same method almost. After the Stock Market Crash of 1929, Hoover refused to launch a program that would give federal aid to the unemployed. The government should stay out of the way. Capitalism, I can dig it. Instead, in 1932, he established the

Reconstruction Finance Corporation. This entity loaned out about two billion dollars to ailing banks, insurance companies and other financial institutions in hopes the money would trickle down.[2]

Two things to look at here, first, the money didn't trickle down. Unemployment continued to skyrocket. His bullshit program had absolutely no stimulative effect on the economy. While he was giving billions to bankers and CEO's, the middle class were literally sleeping in tents. This is the epitome of this bullshit ideology. Second, the unemployed, who were victims of circumstance don't get federal relief. Because capitalism says government should stay out of the way. The rich do get a bailout because the term capitalism has been modified to exclude them from all the rules.

That's the conservative economic ideology. Bailout the rich and hope it trickles down to the middle class that was subjected to living in tents and using newspaper as blankets

After Hoover's failed experiment, trickle-down economics went out of style for a while. Then came F.D.R. and the New Deal. The principle behind the New Deal was practical, and the need for a New Deal was obvious. The middle class and the poor had gotten the shaft.

America's economy was built on capitalism. Government stayed out of the way and gave each individual the liberty to pursue their own happiness. If wealth was that pursuit then so be it. If you failed then tough luck. If you made it then you had the liberty to enjoy your wealth. You could spread it around or you could hoard it all away for yourself. The choice was yours. The thing is, everybody was given a fair shake. After that it was up to you to shape your own destiny.

As the economy grew bigger things became a bit more complicated. For various reasons the economy experienced a number of depressions. There were periods of boom and busts. The busts were turning into big busts and they tended to happen on numerous occasions.

When the economy would experience these temporary catastrophes many Americans suffered. Those Americans suffered through no fault of their own. It was becoming the consequence of a flawed banking system.

The Panic of 1837 is a good example of this. Not long after President Van Buren's inauguration banks in New York City and a few other places suspended the practice of converting paper money into gold and silver. This touched off a nationwide panic that led to a depression which lasted until 1843. The meltdown was brought about for a few converging reasons. Putting the Specie Circular policies into effect. This law was passed by Andrew Jackson. This policy caused a credit crunch. Successive crop failures, and an unfavorable trade balance with England, caused this whole nightmare to take shape. About 900 banks around the country went belly up. The unemployed began rioting for food.[2]

The Great Bank Debate of 1841 led to numerous resignation that year. Everybody realized the need to fix the system, but the methods were far from the same. Then just when it looked like the nation was finally on solid economic footing the Panic of 1857 took place.

The kickoff to this meltdown started because the Ohio Life Insurance Company fell flat on its face. The unexpected death triggered bank runs across the country. The nation went into a depression that lasted until the Civil War . Once again, there was more than one factor for the collapse. Overexpansion of the railroads, operating state banks grew rapidly under bullshit state banking laws, the price of gold began dropping in the wake of The California Gold Rush, and the Crimean War had ended in Europe. This caused governments to cut back on imports of U.S. foodstuffs.

The failure of Jay Cooke & Company kicked off the financial Panic of 1873. This turned into the worse one of all up until that point. It was a five year depression that saw about three million go unemployed in no time. Some of the cause that contributed to the slump were a depression in Europe thanks to the crash in the Vienna Stock Market, overextensions of the railroads, the screwed and depressed state in the insurance industry in the wake of the Great Chicago Fire of 1871, and a string of other fires in other cities. Business failures were at an all-time high. They ended up totaling over a half of a billion dollars.[2]

Congress came with minor reforms over the years after the 1873 meltdown, and for a while it looked like the economy might sustain some momentum for at least a few decades. Keep in mind, these were not just two year recessions. They were depressions, and they were lasting for an average of six years a pop. Then in 1893, the

Philadelphia and Reading Railroad failed. This touched off a panic that was followed by a four year depression. Then of course, there were underlying causes of the depression. Things like, dwindling down gold reserves, industrial overexpansion, crop harvest was a mess in the South and in the West. Once again, Europe's lousy economy played a part as well. Thousands of businesses (including a quarter of the nation's railroads) went bankrupt.[2] It was clear that everybody in the country just had to brace themselves about once every 15 years for economic calamity and hope you could somehow avoid it. Then you had to hope the consequences of these type of meltdowns avoided you.

Once again, Congress tried to put a band-aid on the problem. This time by repealing the Sherman Silver Purchase Act.

In 1901, Teddy Roosevelt set forth his Antitrust Policy. His administration ended up bringing suits under the antitrust laws against the railroads, tobacco, beef, oil, and other companies.[2]

Then came the Elkins Act of 1903 and the Hepburn Act of 1906 strengthening the Interstate Commerce Commission in regulating the railroads. This antitrust policy constituted what he titled the "Square Deal". These types of regulations seemed like a good start and were the signs of a government that slowly started to realize the need for intervention.[2]

Then came the Panic of 1907. The failure of the Knickerbocker Trust Company of New York in October of that year caused a panic that caused a collapse of a dozen other banks and railroads. Stock prices went down the toilet. A recovery would begin in the Spring of 1908. The irony is most critics blamed Roosevelt's antitrust and pro-labor laws for squeezing corporate profits. Roosevelt pointed the finger at big businesses for the mild collapse.[2]

Government was placing more and more regulations in certain areas that at one time were seen as off limits. Like the Mann-Elkins Act of 1910. It not only extended the authority of the Interstate Commerce Commission to fix its own maximum rates by railroads, it also banned the practice of charging more for short hauls than for longer ones. Most notably, it placed regulations on the telephone and telegraph industries.[2] These band-aids still didn't solve the problem of how to prevent economic calamity every once in a while.

The Federal Reserve Act of 1913 was supposed to be that remedy. The Federal Reserve has a great concept. It's designed to make the nation's money supply more flexible. Doing so helps cope with changing economic conditions and actually curbing banking abuses. It established a system of twelve regional banks. The banks are governed by a specially selected board hand-picked by the president. All national, and those state banks who were willing to participate, were required to keep a portion of their capital on deposit at a federal reserve.[2]

The Federal Reserve was also allowed to loan money to member banks. Then the Fed could vary the interest rate or rates giving them a discount rate. The Fed was now able to control credit. Tightening it in boon times, and relaxing it in periods of economic contraction. This helped smooth out wild fluctuations which were pretty common in past business cycles.[2]

The Federal Reserve was a good starting point for ending the era of wacko meltdowns that lasted over a half decade. The Fed when used properly helps stabilize the economy during turbulent times. Of course, we have also come to learn that the Federal Reserve when not used properly tends to <u>cause</u> recessions as a result of bubbles, but more on that later.

Then came the worst depression of all. The one known as the "Great Depression". On Black Thursday, October 24, 1929, the crash came in full force. Billions of dollars in stocks went straight down the toilet. The 16 million shares was a record in volume. The Dow Jones Industrial average plummeted to 41. Far below its 1929 peak of 381.[2]

There were a variety of different causes for the depression. Among others were chronic surpluses in agricultural products had been depressing farm prices. There was also a lack of credit restraints, especially in the securities industry, where stocks were being swooped on for a 25 percent margin. This spurred a frantic round of speculation. Corporate profits accelerated at the expense of higher wages stunted purchasing power. High tariffs also discouraged world trade.[2]

The unemployment rate would skyrocket to 25 percent by 1933. Hoover stood by and did nothing but throw a few billion toward the rich. The economy was turned upside down on its head.

So, Roosevelt came with the New Deal. The New Deal was a reversal of many things and a needed change. One of the principles of the economy was nobody deserved a handout but everybody deserved a fair shake. Much of the middle class and the poor were becoming victims of circumstance. Prior economic depressions were leaving large footprints on current economic cycles. Certain areas of the country were being hit harder by certain depressions. This made it even harder to not only rebuild, but for the people concentrated in certain segments to have the same opportunity as others. This, of course, could be brushed over in the name of politics. After all, people still had a chance. Many had just a slim chance.

The Great Depression of the 1930's was different. It was too big and too widespread to look over. Action had to be taken and a new method had to be tried. For the first time government would bailout the poor and the middle class instead of isolating such help to the people who didn't need it.

Roosevelt didn't take his eyes off the banks. In fact, his first day in office he declared a bank holiday. This was huge. At the time the whole banking industry was in danger of going under. People everywhere were scrambling to get their money out of them a.s.a.p. More than half the banks had gone bankrupt while others suspended privileges.[2]

The bank holiday gave federal auditors a chance to go over the books. The ones that were determined to be sound re-opened. This was a big accomplishment. The bank holiday restored some public confidence and slowed down the bank runs. After helping the banks out, Roosevelt came with some needed regulation. There would be no more band-aids put in place. The banking system didn't need timid reforms. It needed a permanent fix. As a result, a number of regulations were put in place to prevent another depression. There might be recessions here and there, but no more economic calamities. The era of depressions had to be put to rest.

The banking acts of 1933 and 1935 barred banks from dealing in stocks and bonds and established the Federal Deposit Insurance Corporation. Executive orders, in April of 1933, called in gold, forbade its export, and formally took U.S. currency off the gold standard. These were essential first steps in laying the foundation to a stabilized banking system and a sound currency flow.[2]

Then in 1934, the Securities and Exchange Commission was created. The agency was established to correct abuses that led to the Stock Market Crash of 1929. Almost all stocks and bonds traded on the exchanges were to be registered with the SEC. The commission was also given the authority to set margin requirements and regulate securities transactions on the exchanges.[2]

So, for the New Deal, helping the banks wasn't just about a bailout. It was also about correcting the problem for good. If government can intervene and save the asses of the banks, surely it can intervene to make sure that they are following basic rules that not only save them from going belly up, but also save other innocent Americans from losing everything they own.

The New Deal also bailed out the poor and middle class as well. Some of the most notable programs were: The Civilian Conservation Corps (CCC). In 1933, the CCC hired more than 3 million young men ages 18-25. All of them from poor families, mostly from cities, to build roads, plant trees, and work on a number of conservation projects like flood control. They were stationed in camps and placed under military supervision. There was also the Federal Emergency Relief Administration in 1933. This program was designed to administer aid to the poor in various ways.[2]

The Rural Electrification Administration of 1935 was established to provide funds to extend electric power to rural areas that had been neglected by the utility companies because such services was not nearly as profitable as it was in concentrated population areas.[2]

The Works Progress Administration of 1935 was criticized as a "make work scheme". Apparently, the scheme worked. "WPA" employees constructed 125,000 buildings, 650,000 miles of road, 75,000 bridges, along with a crapload of other facilities.[2] Then, of course, there was the Social Security Act of 1935. It created today's modern day social security system.[2] These are just a few of the New Deal programs. The New Deal was not just a moral program that reshaped the social and political landscape. The New Deal was as Clinton said, "an economic program." Federal aid injected into the economy for the poor and middle class.

The safety net was made to give everybody a fair chance, and to ensure that if you worked hard and contributed to this country in an honest and responsible way you wouldn't have to starve to death when you're too old to work. If you helped pay into the system for 45 years then the system should ensure you don't just get a bum deal when you reached a certain age.

The game had already started changing long before the New Deal but government had finally caught on. Bailing out the banks was a necessary evil, but bailing out the middle class and the poor should be considered a necessary good.

As I mentioned in the last chapter, Truman continued with the "Fair Deal". Despite his earlier rhetoric, Dwight Eisenhower didn't touch the New Deal.

In a commencement speech at the University of Michigan, Lyndon B. Johnson declared: "We have the opportunity to move not only toward the rich society and the powerful society, but upward to the great society. The great society rests on abundance and liberty for all. It demands an end to poverty and racial injustice...the great society, it is a place where every child can find knowledge to enrich his mind and to enlarge his talents."

The "Great Society" included the war on poverty, Civil Rights Legislation, Medicare and Medicaid, environmental protection, and consumerism. The Great Society picked right up where the New Deal left off.

Some of Nixon's accomplishments include: the Revenue Sharing Program he adopted that poured billions of tax dollars back into state and local governments, along with the Consumer Product Safety Act of 1972 which created the Consumer Product Safety Commission (This independent regulatory agency set product safety standards and balanced unsafe products from the marketplace).[2] He also made a lot of headway upgrading environmental standards. He signed into law the Environmental Quality Policy Act of 1969. This act required filing for an environmental impact statement for each new program. In 1970, the Nixon Administration would then usher in the era of the Environmental Protection Agency. The "EPA" was created to monitor, reduce, regulate and help control pollution.[2] This is just a few of the several laws Nixon would pass concerning environmental safety standards. When Nixon was in office conservatives praised him and helped him win re-election by a landslide. After his graceless departure however, his policies have been lambasted ever since.

Many of Nixon's policies resemble those of a liberal Democrat, but conservatives didn't give a shit. They were too busy re-electing him. After the one-two punch of Nixon and Ford, conservatives went with their strategy of extreme right.

In came Ronald Reagan, conservatives knew that this was their chance to highjack the party again. Barry Goldwater's radical platform failed to claim victory.

The moderate Nixon worked and they were all for him and his new regulations on the environment and the marketplace. But after him and Ford managed to totally make the party look like stupid lowlifes, they (conservatives) went back to Plan B.

When Ronald Reagan was picked to be the guy to lead the movement, he exemplified everything conservatives were looking for. He was Barry Goldwater and Herbert Hoover on steroids. Ronald Reagan's rhetoric pushed the Republican Party back to conservatives. Reaganites dominated the Republican convention and felt the tactic for radical right gave them their best chance. It was a tactic that they felt comfortable with. The only difference was this time it worked.

Reagan's platform among other things was: a constitutional amendment to ban abortion, increase defense spending, de-control oil and gas prices, dropping the party's longstanding support for an Equal Rights Amendment for Women, a balanced budget, and steep tax cuts. This platform is one the Reaganites have been stuck on ever since. As far as they were concerned this is what made Reagan a winner.

Reagan campaigned as a staunch conservative and nothing reflected his ideology like his economic views. Reagan's economic vision was not original. As mentioned earlier, it was tried in the 1920's by Calvin Coolidge, and the concept was instituted by Herbert Hoover during the Great Depression. After Hoover it was dreamed up in the minds of some other assholes who didn't know shit about economics. It was pretty obvious Barry Goldwater was trying to rekindle the magic, but after his humiliating defeat it took some balls for Reagan to try and assert such an off the wall ideology, but he did it and it won him the White House. What's so incredibly fascinating is how conservatives bought into it and still buy into it.

It's called trickle-down economics. To make it short and as simply stupid as it really is, it works like this. You first cut everybody's taxes, sounds good so far, huh? The thing is, you only cut taxes for the middle class and the poor by a small amount. You cut taxes for the rich <u>a lot</u>. I mean, just give the top 20 percent wealthiest Americans about 75 percent of the tax cuts and let the bottom 80 percent split the other 25 percent. This might sound unfair, but not according to trickle-down economics. You see, when you cut taxes for the rich, it trickles down to everyone else. So, even though the poor and the middle class are not getting much of a tax cut, the riches from above will make its way down. (This is because the rich are known as "job creators" and the rich you see, need huge sums of money to create these jobs.)

Reagan campaigned on cutting taxes by huge amounts. Now when you cut taxes you're reducing revenue for the Treasury. Those tax dollars now disappear. So, Reagan was asked how he was going to pay for the massive tax cuts. Like Bush, Reagan too was a savvy economist. He had a theory tax cuts magically pay for themselves.

This is actually called supply side economics. According to this theory, tax cuts spur investment and improve productivity, which in turn creates more jobs. By providing so many people more jobs the Treasury now has extra tax dollars to collect. This generates so much extra revenue that the budget can be balanced and an economic utopia can begin. Now it's important to note something here. This shit never works.

Reagan might have really believed this crap because he

came into the White House and put supply side economics into effect. Reagan slashed taxes by over 260 billion dollars and did not pay for them. The wealthiest Americans received the largest chunks of the tax cuts.

After giving out the huge tax breaks for the rich, Reagan and other Republicans must have thought this was going to kick start the economy. When Reagan entered the White House the unemployment rate was 7.5 percent. Despite the huge tax breaks the unemployment rate would climb to 10.8 percent. Reagan's approval rating fell to the mid-30's. To make things worse the damn tax cuts didn't pay for themselves.

The economy ended up bouncing back with force which really saved Reagan's ass. The last two years of Reagan's term the economy would expand at a robust rate of about 8 percent. Unemployment would drop to about 7.2 percent by the time he went up for re-election. The thing is Reaganomics had pretty much nothing to do with the robust recovery. What had the economy in such an unstable condition when Reagan took office was inflation. When Reagan took office inflation was at 13 percent. The rate would fall all the way to two percent by 1986.

The Federal Reserve, led by Paul Volcker, had an effective tight money policy that really helped curb inflation and bring it back to control. Now some might say Reagan deserves credit for helping to curb inflation. I think he deserves some credit too.

The point is his stupid ass tax cuts for the rich did

absolutely nothing to stimulate the economy. It was the Federal Reserve that did the heavy lifting, and even after the economy got back on track the tax cuts were still not paying for themselves. In fact, the national debt exceeded one trillion dollars his first year in office. In 1982, the national deficit exceeded 100 billion dollars for the first time. In three of the next four years it would exceed 200 billion for the first time. The damn tax cuts just wouldn't pay for themselves for some reason. So Reagan began hiking taxes. He would go against his campaign promise, but Reagan's tax hikes were some of the slickest, most brazen, underhanded tax hikes in U.S. history. After blowing holes in the deficit to accommodate the rich, Reagan would put the biggest share of the revenue burden on the middle class. It went something like this.[2]

In 1981, Ronald Reagan appointed a lowlife, lying, bug-eyed dickhead named Alan Greenspan to head the National Commission on Social Security Reform.[1] Now there's a long sensational story I could tell about Greenspan, but unless I succumb to temptation it is a story for another book. Just know for the moment he's a lowlife, lying, bug-eyed dickhead. The Great Commission was created because of an alleged crisis.

It seemed short term funding was about to run dry and leave The Old-Age and Survivors Insurance Trust Fund bankrupt by 1983.[1]

Greenspan came with a brilliant idea. He recommended hikes in the Social Security tax. You see, the Social Security tax is not considered a real "tax". That's because the taxpayer will see a return on his dollar in the form of benefits later. Yes, this is supposed to be a real theory.[1]

The rationale behind this little scheme was supposed to be that because a multitude of baby boomers were in their prime at the time, the Reagan Administration could go ahead and hike the payments. This would build up a surplus. The surplus could be used in the next two or three decades to pay out benefits when the boomers reached retirement age and were ready to sit back and enjoy their golden years. The administration liked Greenspan's solution and accepted it. The Social Security tax rate which was 9.35 percent in 1981 went up to 15.3 percent by 1990.[1]

Now this is pretty interesting for a few reasons. The Social Security tax may not be looked at as a real tax, but a real tax it is, and it's regressive. One of the reasons for this is it's only applied to wage income. They are capped at 106,000. This means wages above a certain level are not taxed at all.[1]

So, let's just say hypothetically that Social Security taxes should be momentarily ignored as coming in the form of benefits. If they are looked at as just a source of revenue for the government then this would be just a tax hike on middle class taxpayers who are already kicking out a disappropriate rate. We can't ignore the fact it's coming back as benefits though, right? Well, this is where the scam gets good. You see, Greenspan's plan to build up a war chest for Social Security was nothing but a bunch of bullshit. The war chest was never taken seriously from day one. This fact could lead some to believe that this was never really the intention for the tax hike.[1]

When your tax dollars pay for Social Security they never have gone into a locked box that is separate from the rest of the budget. They have literally been a source of government revenue period. After Greenspan's bright idea was implemented, the Social Security Administration bought T-bills with the money. This neat trick was the vehicle for lending cash back to the government for use on all kinds of other shit that had nothing to do with Social Security. This gave Reagan the power (after he hiked taxes on Social Security) to dig into the budget and take all the Social Security money he wanted for his short term spending spree. Then he left a bunch of government notes or bonds. Basically IOU's. This is exactly what he did too. This massive tax hike on the middle class turns into a gift that kept on giving. 1.69 trillion dollars in regressive taxes over the next 20 years. And yes, the gift kept on giving. When Reagan got away with it, every president after him followed the tradition of raiding Social Security. From Bush (Part 1) to Clinton and then Bush (Part 2).[1]

Bush (Part 2) proved that sequels are always worse. He didn't just spend the money. He spent all the money in Social Security. This led to then Treasury Secretary, Paul O'Neil to announce with great pain: "I come to you as managing trustee of Social Security, today we have no assets in the fund."[1]

Translation:
After funding tax breaks for the rich, we don't have shit in the Social Security Trust Fund except pieces of paper reminding us of all the times we stole your benefits after hiking your taxes to astronomical levels.

Then it gets even more absurd. After the Bush Administration decided to reveal that Social Security tax dollars had been spent on everything but the right thing it was the great genius behind the massive tax hike who came out and offered some more brilliant ideas. Alan Greenspan "bravely" speaks out that it's time to cut Social Security benefits.[1]

The Washington Post reported in February of 2004: Greenspan offered several ways to curtail federal spending growth, including reducing Social Security and Medicare benefits. The Fed Chairman again recommended raising the age at which retirees could become eligible, to keep pace with the population's rising longevity.[1]

The article then goes on to talk about Greenspan's suggestion for curtailing benefits. So, Greenspan and Reagan get together and pull off one of the most clever and one of the biggest tax hikes ever. They justify huge tax hikes on the middle class by promising to take that money and stuff it away safely to be used as benefits. Instead, they use up the money on current government spending. This is so audacious it's amazing.[1]

So after your Social Security tax dollars were spent on tax cuts for the rich and other shit, your benefits should get cut. What's even more unbelievable is that Greenspan's imprint is there from start to finish. He's the guy who hikes Social Security taxes by 1.69 trillion dollars, then he's the same guy who comes out twenty years later and says that the promised benefits can't be paid out.[1]

This method of taxing the middle class and then taking

their money and using it for deficit spending rather than promised benefits earned a pretty popular nickname: A *Ponzi scheme*. This Ponzi scheme raised taxes on the middle class year after year during the 80's so that Reagan could fund his huge deficits. Never once was it given a second thought that the benefits that they're (American people) tax dollars are supposed to be going on would not be there if the government keeps tapping into it for other things.[1]

What's so remarkable is that Reagan, a small government ideologue, would use such government power and deceit to justify hiking taxes while increasing spending more than any president before him. Reagan came out and called these tax hikes — with a straight face — revenue enhancements, because this money comes back as benefits. Then he took the money and spent it on other things the government needed it for. So much for revenue enhancements. The benefits, as stated earlier, could not be afforded and (as of this writing) all Social Security has in it is a bunch of IOU's.[1]

While taxes were being raised every year on the middle class, with Reagan signing off on it with every budget, he would come with sweeping tax reform in 1986. Reagan would sign into law the Gramm-Rudman-Hollings Act which set deficit reduction targets. This too would provide the rich with a huge windfall.[2] Rich people were happy. Despite eleven tax hikes during his two terms, Reagan managed to rekindle his love affair with the rich. This love affair would leave his successor with massive deficits.

So, first Reagan comes with the largest tax cut known to mankind when he comes into office. The cuts are tailored toward the rich. Unemployment climbs rapidly his first year in office to double figures. After his first two years in office Reagan is extremely unpopular, burdened with a lousy economy and huge deficits. Reagan decides to say to hell with this and begins hiking taxes. When the inflation rate drops, the economy roared back to life. Despite the economic renaissance the tax cuts still didn't pay for themselves and not even his tax hikes were plugging the holes in the deficit. Even while raiding Social Security and kicking the middle class dead in their asses, Reagan couldn't get the deficit under control.

Reaganomics was extremely flawed at best. There is no doubt the Reagan Administration deserved a lot of credit for taming inflation, even if it was the Federal Reserve that did all the work.

It still happened under Reagan's watch. The fall of the inflation rate led to robust economic growth and millions of new jobs. The tax cuts did nothing to spur such growth. They were passed with great fanfare and despite the huge sums of money going back into the pockets of the rich people, the unemployment rate climbed to 10.8 percent. The robust economic growth of the 80's coincided with the drop of the inflation rate but not with the tax cut package.

Even more telling, the deficits swelled to record levels despite the strong job growth. So it's clear supply side economics works in a perfect world—maybe—but it does not have positive results in the real world. Even Reagan's own tax hikes could not make a dent in the deficits. According to the "Tax Foundation", a Washington based private research group that monitors government fiscal policy, estimated that the overall tax burden on the average American worker was either little changed or slightly worse during the Reagan years.[2]

Federal spending as a percentage of gross domestic product increased.[2] And how was he financing all that spending? With the massive tax hikes I mentioned earlier, not just the social security tax hike but *eleven* other tax hikes that conservatives to this day deny even exists . Those tax hikes are: Tax Equity and Fiscal Responsibility Act of 1982, Highway Revenue Act of 1982, Social Security Amendments of 1983, Railroad Retirement Revenue Act of 1983, Deficit Reduction Act of 1984, Consolidated Omnibus Budget Reconciliation Act of 1985, Omnibus Budget Reconciliation Act of 1985, Superfund Amendments and Reauthorization Act of 1986, Continuing Resolution for 1987, Omnibus Budget Reconciliation Act of 1987 and the Continuing Resolution for 1988. The total cumulative amount of these tax increases come to 132.7 billion dollars. Yet despite all those tax hikes, the next fact is a painful reality for supporters of Reaganomics. It is the icing on the cake.

Thanks to his spending spree and massive tax cuts for the wealthy, The United States, under Reagan, went from being the largest *creditor* nation to being the largest *debtor* nation. A real staunch fiscal conservative, huh? This is their small government hero in a nutshell. These same Reaganites protest under the moniker of Tea Party and have the audacity to act like they really give a shit about government spending. Listen to them tell it, Reagan was a budget balancing machine. The sad part is that they know better. They actually try to deceive the rest of the electorate with this little game they play. These are the same people who refused to raise the debt ceiling. Where were they for the multitude of times Reagan raised it? Where were they when Reagan warned of the consequences of not raising the debt ceiling?

They care nothing about Reagan's record, just his rhetoric. They heard Reagan yell at Congress about a balanced budget amendment, but he never bothered to submit one himself. I guess it was hard to submit a balanced budget when he was paying an annual interest on the debt of 150 billion dollars. That was the third largest item in the budget. The debt had almost tripled under Reagan so it's only natural that the interest rate would swell so big.

George H.W. Bush campaigned as a fiscal conservative who was going to bring the deficit below 35 billion dollars without raising taxes. Once again, the conservative economic ideology made for good sound bites but it never matches reality. When Bush took office he came to the realization that the massive deficits left by Reagan were too big to overcome without tax increases. His new position really pissed off conservatives. They were hoping he could have at least been discreet like Reagan. Reagan never made public announcements. He went behind closed doors, compromised on taxes, and then signed the legislation into law a few days later. That was the end of that. Not Bush, he wants to be open and honest all of a sudden. When Bush raised taxes, he **raised** taxes. He didn't miss a beat. He raised taxes on gasoline, cigarettes, beer, etc. He might as well have tagged Little Debbies and SpongeBob Squarepants products too. A lot of revenue could have come from that. Hell, a tax on SpongeBob alone might have erased the deficit. If SpongeBob even existed. If not, Barbie dolls would have been a real ace in the hole.

Anyway, as stated earlier, Bush lost re-election. The lousy economy was just lousy all throughout his term. From his first day in office the economy really did suck. Then even before the tax hikes could be considered part of the reason, businesses went to dropping off one by one. In fact, more businesses failed under Bush than any president in U.S. history.

The country then tipped into a recession despite feeling like it was supposed to be time for a recovery. Believe it or not, the economy started to improve a bit in his last year in office, and if not for Ross (deformed-eared, funny-faced) Perot he might have won re-election. Perot stole 19 percent of the popular vote. Bush was already going to be in a struggle with the economy still sluggish. Perot basically sealed the fate of Bush while becoming the best sideshow in years for voters.

Then came the Clinton era, Clinton's economic policy would not only be a stunning success, but it would spit in the face of conservative economics. The economy ran like a well-oiled machine throughout the Clinton era while disproving the tax myth once and for all.

When Republicans decided to shut the government down in November of 1995, they not only overplayed their hand, they exposed just how warped and out of touch their world view is. Republican amendments in their budget included among other things: to limit appeals by death row inmates, make it harder to issue health, safety and environmental regulations, bar illegal immigrants from education facilities, and deep cuts to Medicare, Social Security and education. Cutting these programs would also help finance another round of tax cuts for the rich.

Of course Clinton rejected the budget. And as you know, the whole country told Republicans to flush that stupid ass budget proposal. Once again, this is another example of economics being used to pursue a social agenda. Through "one" budget, Republicans wanted to reform entitlements, cut every program they didn't like and express just who they felt were a priority to the county and who was just a burden. They were willing to hike premiums on Medicare, but use that hike to finance a tax cut for some millionaires. Clinton decided to do the opposite. He protected programs for the poor and middle class, and in his first year in office raised taxes by over 280 billion dollars.

Conservatives went absolutely ape shit. They figured the tax hikes would probably tip the economy into a recession. Instead, the budget had an extremely positive effect, and yes the rich –gasp- had to pay a whole lot more in taxes…Aghhh!!! We're not gonna make it!!! That's right. Just pause and catch your breath. Clinton not only raised taxes on the middle class. He raised them on the rich. I mean hiked them too. The rich then fled the country in protest, after which we were all forced to cry out for mercy because we looked like a poor version of France. No, that didn't happen. What really happened was the rich evaded their tax obligation forcing the Treasury into a crisis as deficits swelled to the point that we went bankrupt and had to go ahead and sell Texas to China. Okay, that didn't happen either. What really happened was that for the first time in years the Treasury had more revenue than it had ever seen.

This strange new flow of revenue led to the deficit not only shrinking but completely disappearing. Because there were no deficits, surpluses were being used to not only pay down the national debt, but to also put money back into the economy. Clinton had this strange idea that if the Treasury has enough revenue, and the government actually makes *responsible* cuts in spending that doesn't harm children and the poor along with the rest of the economy, that this would lead to healthy economic growth. Talk about crazy, huh? What happened to the good old days under Reagan when deficits didn't mean shit?

After the massive tax hikes, an economic boom took place. By the end of January 2000, economist were dumbfounded to see the unemployment rate drop to a 30 year low. Up until that point, full employment was looked at as being five percent. Many figured that was about as good as it gets. It seemed unrealistic to think the economy would ever reach the heights it did during the sixties. The economy under Clinton not only reached those heights, it surpassed them.

In February 2000, the economy set a record for the longest sustained expansion in history. At one point the unemployment rate would fall under four percent.[2] An unprecedented achievement. During Clinton's two terms more jobs were added to payrolls then at any point in U.S.

history. Over 21 million jobs, even though the "job creators" were faithfully paying taxes. And the budget...Clinton proved that although tax cuts don't really pay for themselves, taxes themselves *pay off*. The extra tax dollars wiped out the Reagan-Bush deficits. At the end of 1999, the U.S. budget surplus was 100 billion dollars. It was the first surplus in decades. Clinton's four straight balanced budgets are a record. Because of the balanced budgets the U.S. was chipping away at its debt which was lowering the interest rate on the debt. This was freeing up more money for trivial things. Stuff like...the economy! The annual surplus Clinton left behind was 230 billion dollars. The Congressional Budget Office predicted that Clinton's last budget would lead to a 5.6 trillion surplus over the next decade. Imagine that. Our national debt in 2011 might have been around 1 trillion dollars instead of sneaking up to 15 trillion.

Clinton balanced the budget and refused to do it on the backs of the poor. He didn't cut into Medicare, Social Security, education or the environment.

He made some sensible cuts, and he raised taxes in the middle of an economic recovery. A recovery that would turn into the strongest economic era on record. When those taxes got hiked on the rich they didn't run. They prospered. When some of the extra revenue was being reinvested back into the economy it sparked growth which caused a lot of that investment to be used to hire, which turned into a supply flow that triggered demand which contributed to a robust cycle. The rich didn't make the middle class wealthy. Instead the middle class made the wealthy very rich. The rich prospered thanks to a robust middle class. The middle class is what built America's economy, not the other way around. This was proven during the Clinton era. The more the middle class expanded the stronger the economy got. This is not only about what's right. It's about what's smart and what's practical. It's about what's worked time and again and what has failed time and again.

If Republicans cold-heartedly disregarded the middle class and the poor in the name of nuts and bolts, sound economics I could understand. I might not like it, but I could understand. What baffles me is that they shit on the middle class and the poor in the name of an economic policy that has been nothing but a proven failure at best. You would think the Clinton era would have been a great lesson to look over for any of his replacements. Ideology should not be clung to when it doesn't match reality. Clinton pissed liberals off when he reformed welfare, yet, most people consider the reform to be a success. Conservatives loved it, but conservatives along with many other Americans hate the fact that Clinton hiked taxes, but these same people cheered when they saw that the tax hikes didn't even cause a glitch in the economy. They also cheered when they realized the extra revenue was being used to spit out balanced budgets one year after another. Clinton did try to push his ideology his first two years in office, but when he shifted to the center it was a new ballgame. It came natural for him to govern as a moderate. As a moderate, he refused to back down on his tax hikes and was unwavering on welfare reform. He was not chained to an ideology.

Clinton also showed that the tax hikes alone would not

be enough. So, he came with "PAYGO". The tax hikes helped get him in reach of a balanced budget, but spending properly is a different story. You see, Clinton understood what was common sense to most normal hard working Americans. He understood that government should actually "pay" for what it buys.

Any bills signed into law had to be paid for. So, he was not just collecting more money though tax hikes, he was spending it responsibly. Please keep in mind that what's common sense to most normal Americans is rocket science to our government at times. Not because our elected officials lack intellect. But because they sometimes lack courage and use this cowardice to come off like bravely stubborn patriots who are in actuality assholes.

So, the country prospered under Clinton's economic vision. Then came Bush (Part 2). As predicted, the sequel is always worse than the first. Despite the fact that Clinton left behind an annual surplus, Bush insisted all throughout his campaign that he was going to be the "tax cutting person" he was during his glory days as governor of Texas. You see, Bush wanted to make sure that the nation prospered the way Texas prospered after his bold tax cuts. When Bush was governor of Texas he really slashed taxes. One of the taxes he lowered was the property tax.

The Dallas Morning News, however, seemed to think his tax cuts actually had a negative effect. According to the newspaper's analysis, many Texans were still paying as much in taxes as they were in 1997, or more.[2]

It seems that when Bush lowered the property taxes he

didn't take into account that local districts might lose revenue. He probably missed such a common sense point because tax cuts are supposed to pay for themselves. Local districts throughout the state ended up having to raise taxes which left people paying the same or more. Bush overlooked these inconvenient facts and boldly carried on preaching his economic vision throughout the campaign.

When Bush won the White House, the "compassionate conservative" came with a huge tax cut...for the rich. I guess that's a sign of compassion. The 1.35 trillion dollar package had a 10 year life span. This compassionate conservative tax cut cost a whole lot, but according to who you ask, the tax cuts seemed to target only one class of people. President Bush proudly asserted that the "vast majority of my tax cuts are for the bottom end of the spectrum."[2] This statement doesn't mean Bush is just a lying sack of horseshit. Independent studies have found that Bush's brain only registered to a certain degree and then would experience some type of malfunction when trying to see something outside of that reality. It seems Bush might have actually thought the richest ten percent were the only people in the country!

Regardless, there was actually no fact whatsoever to his bullshit assertion. As stated earlier, the Tax Policy Center, along with the Congressional Budget Office, and other independent studies all came to the same conclusion. The tax cuts were for the rich. The bottom 60 percent of the economy received crumbs. The top 10 percent of the country got the biggest chunk.

Then there were forecasters from everywhere warning

Bush about the flawed package. In 2003, 450 economist from the U.S. along with ten Noble Laureates, warned the idiot that the tax cuts would not help the economy in the short run, and the projected deficits would do a lot of harm over the long haul.[2]

Now imagine that for a moment and digest it if you can. *450* economist (all in the U.S.) are on one accord telling Bush that this is not going to help the economy in the short run and it will hurt it in the long run. If 450 economist said anything negative about an Obama proposal, all of them would have one month contracts on Fox News. Fox would work them 12 to 16 hours a day on each talk show and then the Tea Party would take to the street in mass protest with disturbing billboards. It would be utter chaos. Here's the kicker though. It would be understandable—except for the racist ass billboards. 450 U.S. economist and ten Nobel Laureates telling the president to pump his brakes is enough for any voter to get worried. The thing is that didn't happen in the case of George W. Bush. There was no Tea Party taking to the streets and Fox News didn't even mention the shitload of economist telling this guy that this was a bad idea.

Now one still has to ask, why didn't President Bush take heed to all these experts? What did he feel he knew that they didn't? What made him so sure that the tax cuts were such a good idea that he would simply tell all those experts to fuck off? What kind of arrogance does it take to jeopardize an entire country for the sake of being right? This wasn't just some hostile liberals telling the president he loves rich people and he's a jerk. These were experts from all over the country. Experts can be wrong. They can even be biased at times but 450 _and_ some Nobel Laureates? What did this clown base his decision on? Was it proven to work? Every other time it was tried it left deficits and there's no solid data that trickle-down economics even trickles down. The tax rates of the 90's seemed to have worked out just fine for the economy. Why tinker with something that's working? This was like someone saying the car engine I have is already doing a great job, but I have a desire for this other one that's made for a different model. 450 mechanics warn you that the engine you have picked is going to harm your car. Even though you don't know shit about being a mechanic except for some basic fundamentals, you decide to let every last one of those silly mechanics know that they can go straight to hell. Don't you hate mechanics? All they want to do is _fix_ cars.

This is what Bush did. He chose ideology over reality. He chose to double down instead of adapting. He chose to brush off those stupid experts. What did they know? All of them, unanimous with the same opinion. Did he just not care or was he too proud to admit that his package should be repealed? Whatever it was he didn't put the people of this country first, that's for sure. It's not like hindsight is the only factor. He was being warned about these tax cuts in 2003 at a time when the shitty results were just beginning to manifest.

To make matters even worse, some of the same visible flaws that popped up when he was governor of Texas were now rearing their ugly head on a national level. When he was governor of Texas, his tax cuts hurt local districts and forced them to raise taxes because of shortfalls in their budgets. That was on a state level. You would think he would have took heed to such flaws before implementing this policy on a national level. He didn't.

Local governments began complaining about how they had to hike taxes and do a shitload of reducing when it came to services and benefits. They were getting less money from Washington while simultaneously being hit with having to pay for unfunded mandates. According to the non-partisan Center of Budget and Policy Priorities, "Federal policies are costing states and localities about 185 billion over the four year course of the state fiscal crisis."[2] That analysis was made during his first term. Is this a coincidence, or didn't we see this before on the state level in Texas right before he took the White House?

Now, it could be almost understandable that Bush tried to use the same economic formula despite it not producing the desired results on the state level. Hey, just because it failed once doesn't mean it will fail again. Maybe, there was some type of other unseen mitigating factors at hand. Then it's not producing the desired results on the national level either. In fact, the results are looking strangely similar. Then economist and experts come out of the woodwork warning you and then history shows this method creates whopper size deficits. What is the excuse? There is none. It simply goes right back to the point I was making before. Conservatives insist on doubling down on the same failed policies in hopes that at some point it looks like they worked. Then it's vindication. Then it's I told you so. The sad part is while they try to prove a point Americans suffer. The wealth gap in this country is not a product of capitalism. It's a product of morons trying to impose an idea. They have an idea that seems to make sense. Who cares if it's never worked? This shit could happen. If the stars align just right then this just might one day work. If it doesn't, it's just a product of capitalism.

As for those experts who told Bush his tax cuts would do no good to the economy while setting the country up for fiscal harm...well, they must all be undercover liberals. Possibly communist sympathizers who want to "handcuff" the good old boy from Texas, and hold him back from being the true conservative that he is. That's the thing about a true conservative, he doesn't need some East Coast elitist to tell him how to govern a superpower. In this case, it must have been "450" East Coast elitist all crammed up at a secret location in Boston conspiring how to cause Bush to fail so they could blast John Kerry all over the airwaves while the liberal media showers him with praise. This is the kind of conspiracy theories conservatives tend to get entangled in when an expert or the media disagree with them. It's the Joe McCarthy syndrome.

Well as you already know, the experts who warned Bush were right. After his first term the deficit was over 400 billion dollars. Amazingly, the tax cuts—once again—didn't pay for themselves. See the picture here? When Bush inherits the White House he has a big fat 230 billion dollar annual surplus left behind by Clinton. Within one year he erases that surplus and creates a 158 billion dollar deficit. Every year going forward the deficits get bigger. After his first term, the deficit is over 400 billion dollars. By the time his second term ended he would leave his successor a trillion-plus deficit.

And how about that economy? You remember, the money was supposed to trickle down from the rich a.k.a. "job creators'? According to the Bureau for Labor by October of 2004, there was a net job loss since Bush took office of between 600,000 to 800,000 jobs based on a payroll survey. Some surveys taken did contradict and support this number. All of them, however, admitted that the payroll survey had the most accuracy when it came to measuring job losses.[2]

Bush is not just a perfect example of trickle-down economics, he's the latest. It's all the same with this ideology. If you see it once, you have seen it a thousand times. From Coolidge and Hoover to Reagan and Bush. It's an ideology that assumes some type of perfect sequence that is almost incapable of happening in the real world. It's just a fantasy.

According to some basic well-known facts, this theory doesn't work. Then there is the common sense factor. Let's do like conservatives for just a moment and dummy this thing all the way down. The mass majority of the time when you cut a rich person's taxes they stockpile it. This has been a well-known fact over the last few years of the recovery. Corporations have amassed over 1 trillion dollars in wealth that they are just sitting on. They have no desire to start spending it on employees. For what? They are scoring huge profits with the help they got. Extra cash is not a motivation for rich people to just throw it at the economy. They sit on their wealth until they feel it's profitable to invest. Just giving the rich extra money does nothing to motivate them to go on a hiring or spending spree.

When you give a tax cut to someone who's middle class or poor it tends to be a stimulant for the economy because they turn right around and spend the money back into the economy. Most middle class and poor people could use some extra cash, and when they get it they don't play games. They spend. That's because many middle class and poor people don't have the luxury of just sitting on cash. If they did they wouldn't be considered poor and probably not middle class either. These type of people spend that money back into the economy out of necessity. They need goods and services, etc. So, giving these type of people an extra tax cut does make some sense. In fact, the payroll tax cut for the middle class that Congress just renewed for a year will cost about 72 billion dollars, but it's estimated by economist to help create a few hundred thousand jobs. Now that's a "job creator".

When the poor and middle class are able to spend more money that starts a chain reaction within the economy. When they are buying, that triggers demand and when there's demand businesses and corporations are forced to supply more, and many times quicker. When their supply flow is not meeting demand this forces them to seek help in meeting it, which leads to hiring. They don't mind hiring either, because the added customers who are forcing such demand are making them a lot of money. This is what creates job. Not tax cuts for the rich people. A very simple scheme called supply and demand. The key is to increase demand. Rich people are going to spend when they feel like it. So what they're demanding stays the same. But poor and middle class Americans are going to demand more when they can. This is a shot in the arm for the economy when they have such a chance.

Remember a key fact: 70 percent of economic growth is based on consumer spending. Some countries like China for instance, are export economies. Their economy's main source of expansion is through exports. Not the U.S., our main source of economic growth is through consumption. This is one of the main reasons consumer spending is the life blood of our economy. The mass majority of consumers in the U.S. are not rich. Many of us live off a tight budget to survive. When this mass majority of consumers has more money to spend this can trigger a cycle of healthy economic growth.

This is another *common sense* reason it's so important to have a thriving middle class, because the majority of the consumers in our country are considered middle class. Again, when they are spending money it boosts the entire economy. This makes the rich even richer than they would have been without that tax cut. It also saves the government money. In fact, it nudges the government out of the way and lets the market work.

This is another reason many economist frown on cutting unemployment benefits. Many economist and politicians agree that giving someone one dollar in unemployment benefits is like two dollars being put right back into the economy. This is considered one of the most cheapest, traditional stimulant packages around. When Republicans threatened to let these benefits expire because they were not paid for, many economist felt that at least 250,000 jobs could be subtracted from early predictions. The jobs numbers were actually bigger than that among many other economist.

The unemployment benefits not only helped stimulate the economy because it put money into the pockets of consumers, but it helped people who by no fault of their own lost their job because of this recession. Before I go any further on the economic aspect of the unemployment benefits I really have to point something out. It takes a lot of balls for Republicans to get on television and radio and say that they don't like extending unemployment benefits because they are an incentive not to work. They encourage people to sit on their asses and collect a check. First of all, let's try and stick with this theme about common sense. Common sense does help all understand that some people just want to kick back, watch daytime talk shows and collect a check. This is true.

Common sense also says that over 90 percent of these people would rather have a job. There is evidence for such an assumption.

In this last recession, over 8 million jobs were lost. Of those eight million, over 60 percent had been working for at least six months when they lost their jobs. Over half had been employed for at least a year or longer. Many of these people had a steady job for five, ten, fifteen years straight. Oh I get it, these slick folks were waiting on a good recession to come along so they could sit on their suddenly born again lazy asses and collect taxpayer money. Millions, over half according to most surveys, made at least three times more than they are making now. The average unemployment check is about 310.00 a week. Do you really think that someone who is making six, seven, eight or nine hundred dollars a week for ten years straight is now suddenly content to live on three times less? Do these clowns have any idea how hard it is to adjust your budget to such a drastic reduction?

Somehow, because there is an *extremely small* minority of people who will game the system, unemployment benefits are an incentive not to work. I hate to break the news, but if someone is that lazy and has no ambition but to collect a government check then they are going to find a way to do so, with or without unemployment benefits. That's right, newsflash folks, someone who is trying to get out of finding a job is not going to work. Republicans act like that's some type of tough love. Forcing those type of people off of unemployment benefits just inspires them to use other methods. Meanwhile, the mass majority of Americans who need the benefits because they can't get hired are treated like a burden. It's a double standard. Imagine conservatives using the same logic on Wall St. It would go like this, "Even though the mass majority of bankers are probably good people, we don't want to encourage the rotten little crooks scattered around you to do this again. So, we're not bailing you out. We know it might help the economy if we did, but this is tough love." Even though unemployment benefits are a middle class bailout that really does help the economy, conservatives would not want to risk helping those few lazy ones. Wall St. gets TARP. The middle class get a lot of finger wagging and political posturing. This is backwards economic logic.

Even worse it's immoral. It's government turning its back on the people who deserve it and need it. Any dipshit moron, Wall St. ass-kissing puppet who says unemployment benefits should be cut because they are an incentive not to work should be forced to listen to six hours of Sarah Palin trying to justify why she repeatedly botched the story of Paul Revere. This agonizing treatment could possibly be life changing, especially when she gets to the part about everybody else in the world…is mistaken. She knows *for a fact* that Paul went and told those stubborn red coats: No! You're not gonna take our guns" or "regulate our market". Quite a girl, isn't she? Anyway, most people who make such idiotic statements about unemployment benefits are a bit out of step with folks who tragically lost their jobs after 10 or 15 years without warning. Maybe they can't relate to the fact that these people really didn't want to get fired. That had it not been for an economic down turn they would still be (gasp) working. What a revelation, huh?

This common sense stuff is all somehow overlooked. This is not just some liberal bleeding heart rhetoric. This is facts. The facts are, the middle class is the driver of the U.S. economy and in order for this economy to get back to full force it can only go as far as the middle class takes it. If conservatives really love the rich then they will get out of the way of progress, and let them make a bundle of money off a thriving middle class.

5 | SPENDING CUTS AND THE IDIOTS WHO NEVER USE THEM

Trickle-down economics—tax cuts for the rich—is supposed to coincide with spending cuts and deregulation. Tax cuts for the rich is the cornerstone of their economic ideology. Those tax cuts when combined with spending cuts and deregulation is supposed to spark the economy and start a cycle of prosperity the world has never known. I am tempted to skip the part about spending cuts since Republicans **never** cut spending when they are in power. Reagan, Bush (Part 1), and Bush (Part 2) all left behind massive deficits, and all of them spent taxpayer money excessively. When they are *not* in power is when they talk of spending cuts with a religious intensity. It almost makes you wonder what their motives are. Ronald Reagan campaigned and promised that he would produce a balanced budget. We see that was a joke. G.H.W. Bush did the same and blew the deficit to record levels as if he felt the need to outdo Reagan. Bush (Part 2)…well, we already know what he did.

Another good example of the Republican tradition is Paul Ryan. He's a Republican congressman from Wisconsin. He has become the conservative leader of economics. His "brave" budgets have caused conservatives to salivate at the mouth. Many hope he will be vice president or maybe even president one day. His budgets are so...typical. Tax cuts for the rich and just defecate on everybody else. The thing is Paul Ryan has never given a shit about spending until Barack Obama became president. This could be because he admires Obama so much that he wanted to impress him with his new budgets, or it could be that he wanted the new guy to pay him some attention. Or it could be that he's sort of full of shit.

What we do know is that Paul Ryan has never even come close to looking like a fiscal conservative since he's been in Congress. His record is lengthy too. He voted for the Bush tax cuts, both unpaid wars, that damn prescription drug program—which was not paid for at about 400 billion dollars—and every budget that George W. Bush signed into law. The last fact is significant and very rarely (if ever) mentioned. Every budget that George Bush produced increased spending from the previous budget and was financed by deficits that were increasing every year. That's what Paul Ryan was voting for every year. He had no problem with Bush's spending spree.

I have to ask, why was Paul Ryan voting for this unpaid spending spree for eight straight years and now suddenly he's a fiscal conservative? You mean to tell me, he didn't have the spine to stand up to Bush, but he grew one when Obama took office. This doesn't add up.

What's really glaring is that Republicans held majorities in both the House and Senate for almost five years of the Bush presidency.

If Paul Ryan and the other fiscal conservatives wanted to reshape the fiscal picture why didn't they do it at a time when they had the best chance for getting it done? Instead of putting his bold vision before the country at a time when Republicans had the power to do so, he waits until Democrats control the Senate and the White House. Is it because it slipped his mind for about eight years? Instead, he happily voted year after year for bloated budgets and programs that blew the roof off the deficit. He even voted for the last Bush budget which pushed the deficit over 1 trillion dollars. Wow, this guy is brave. He's an economic guru whose determined to bring fiscal sanity back to America. Yeah right.

I could have *almost* understood the excuse that America was not in the fiscal crisis it's in right now, and that's why the sense of urgency has grown so much. Except for one problem. What constitutes a fiscal crisis? According to my calculations, Bush wiped a surplus out his first year in office. When the deficit tipped over 400 billion dollars at the end of 2004, alarm bells were already sounding. Then the deficit went over a half trillion. No urgency yet? What about when Bush turned in a budget that requested 2.9 trillion dollars in spending despite the U.S. having only 2.2 trillion in collected revenue. That's a deficit of 700 billion. Nobody saw the sense of urgency? Nobody felt we were in a fiscal crisis?

Bush pushed the deficit and the debt to record levels and not a peep. Now there is an appeal for fiscal sanity.

Paul Ryan is continuing the tradition of a long line of Republicans before him. Blow the deficit sky high when you're in power then complain like hell that the new Democrat in power is not fixing the problem fast enough.

Paul has come with some pretty bullshit recycled ideas in his last budget. He wants to turn Medicare into a voucher program, Medicaid into a block program, cut into student loan programs, cut into education, cut into environmental protection, etc...and cut taxes for the rich. All that cutting and the rich get tax breaks they don't need. He's not the only one who's a born again cutter. Mitch McConnell of Kentucky is a Republican senator who loved earmarks the way David Vitter loved prostitutes. He's done an about face over the last few years and vows to bring spending under control. Guess what his top priority was at the start of 2011? It was...the deficit? Nope, not the deficit. It was...jobs? No, not jobs. His top priority was "to make Barack Obama a one term president." Several times he made this patriotic statement. I don't know about you, but I sleep better every night knowing Mitch is worrying about Obama instead of the economy, the deficit, the poor, etc.

What a jackass, huh? All the problems this country is facing and he's worried about a campaign two years before the election. If Mitch is that worried about making Obama a one term president then he has to *make* it a priority that the economy and the deficit problem does not get solved under his watch. To *make* him a one term president, he has to *make* sure he fails. If he fails, the American people suffer. But who cares? Normal everyday Americans are just collateral damage. It's nothing personal. It's all about power. That's all this born again budget cutter really cares about. He too has a voting record that mirrors Paul Ryan, Eric Cantor, John Boehner, and a bunch of other born again cost cutters in Congress.

It's sickening to watch these people preach fiscal restraint when these are the same people who voted to do away with fiscal restraint. Never once did they say: Hey Mr. Bush, we like you and everything, we even voted to wipe out the largest annual surplus in U.S. history, but the deficits are starting to rattle us. How about some spending cuts now? No, they didn't do that.

It's almost as sickening as hearing that guy I just mentioned, David Vitter , preach about family values. He's a hypocrite across the board. He loved voting for unpaid tax cuts and unpaid programs the way he loved paying for prostitutes. All the while preaching fiscal restraint and moral standards for America. Talk about a real flip flopper.

They use the whole "we need to cut spending" battle cry as campaign lingo. That's it. Fox News gives these idiots a platform, and lets them blast the airwaves with this whole backwards ass nonsensical rhetoric. What's even more comical is that while these are the same people who blew the deficit to epic proportions they are preaching deficit reduction at a time when economic growth should be the first priority. Amazingly, the media and much of the country take these assholes seriously. This would be like taking your neighborhood preacher seriously in church after you just saw him and David Vitter leaving a hotel with two hookers. You would see him as a hypocrite.

Many conservatives try to justify this newfound faith in spending cuts by saying the Tea party is in town now. They're going to make sure a new day has dawned and that these Republicans will exercise fiscal restraint at all costs. As I pointed out earlier, the Tea Party has always been around during this modern era of politics. These are Reaganites who backed Newt, and supported Bush. They get disgruntled when their guy is not in power. Once a Republican is in office then the deficits will be overlooked.

Now, let's go ahead for a moment and pretend that these are not the same jerkoffs who created these deficits. Let's just hear them out for a second. They want to cut spending and they want to do it now. First, let me give you a little history on what happens when Republicans cut spending. Oh I forgot, I can't. Sorry about that. They have always *increased* spending. But back to the point. They want to cut it now.

Well, cutting spending is not a bad thing. What's stupid is cuts that would hurt an economy that is still fragile. You see, whenever you cut spending you're taking money out of the economy. Conservatives have actually been preaching that spending cuts will help the economy. This is really a bold faced lie. That logic did not come from an economic expert. It comes from a real live jackass.

Conservatives know if they get the public to buy into this crap it puts the president in a tight spot. If he doesn't cut spending right now then he looks like an irresponsible big government liberal. If he does put serious cuts in the budget he would risk slowing down the recovery and Republicans can laugh at what an idiot he is.

To cut spending in the middle of an economic recovery is like the doctor telling his recovering patient to quit taking his life-saving medication so he can heal faster. It's backwards.

Remember, consumer spending is 70 percent of our economy. When the government cuts spending they are cutting it from somewhere that's going to hit either middle class or poor consumers. For example, let's say they cut unemployment benefits. That's a few billion that will not be spent in the economy. It was taken directly out of the pockets of people who were going to spend it. Let's say the government then cuts some money from Planned Parenthood. That's 5 million women who can no longer spend an extra 400 to 800 dollars back into the economy. Do the math. Even if they are only saving 100 dollars a month, thanks to services provided by Planned Parenthood, that would still be over a half billion cut from the economy.

When this extra spending cash is taken from consumers it causes serious contraction. People become scared to spend the little they do have and they start cutting back on spending.

When people cut back it slows down demand. When

demand slows down there's no urgency to supply. When supply starts exceeding demand in such a way companies have to lay people off to keep the balance sheets intact, this creates a cycle in the economy. Now instead of the economy growing, it's going in reverse. Consumers start cutting back because of the budget cuts or because they have now been fired. To help break these type of cycles many economist recommend an infusion of cash. When the money flow is slowing (consumer spending) the economy is shrinking. When money is circulating at a higher rate then this causes the economy to start expanding. This new expansion usually tips the economy back into a new direction that leads to a whole new cycle.

Conservatives have always tried the infusion of cash through tax cuts. Not a bad idea. Lowering taxes does put more money back into the people's pockets. The problem is a huge chunk of the cuts go to people who *don't* need the extra money so they're not going to spend more. The people who *do* need the money are not going to spend more because the tax cut they're getting is so chicken shit small that it's just as well they didn't get a tax cut at all.

The point is, even conservatives still have enough sense to know that consumers needed extra cash to stimulate the economy

Both parties have had their own method, but the main objective was always understood. The economy was in need of extra cash. Now conservatives want spending cuts at this moment. If spending cuts are put into practice right now—I mean real cuts—it could be a serious blow to the economy. You can have a big deficit with a strong economy, but you can't have a balanced budget with a weak economy.

The main objective is to put the country back on sound footing and a path to a balanced budget. The thing is with so many people still out of work, the Treasury does not have the revenue it needs to bring the budget back into balance. More people with jobs means more taxpayers, which means more revenue. Therefore nursing the economy back to life should be the top priority. Here's the gut shot though. That means *increased* spending, not *decreased* spending. It's not sexy but it's got teeth. The economy needs money to grow. Any politician who says he's going to create jobs by cutting spending is full of shit.

That's like telling someone who's dying of thirst that the best way to rehydrate is not to drink any water. It completely defeats and downright spits in the face of rational thinking.

IF the government tries to make serious cuts in the budget now with high unemployment it would be a remedy for a bigger deficit. By slowing down the recovery it forces more would be taxpayers to stay out of the work force, and the ones who are paying taxes might have to cut back on their spending. If the flow of currency shrinks bad enough that could lead to a double dip recession. If that happens and more taxpayers are laid off then that's less revenue for the Treasury. You see the point?

The goal has to be the needed revenue first. You're not going to see a balanced budget with an unemployment rate over eight percent. You have an excellent chance of seeing one with an unemployment rate of five percent though. So you invest in the economy. As of this writing, the economy is growing slowly but surely. It had about three straight months of decent job growth. Over 245,000 a month on average was much better. To risk slowing that down would be stupid.

Our government right now is like someone who's extremely overweight saddled with a pot belly better known as—a huge deficit. If you try to force this person to lose 200 pounds in one week you kill them—*cut spending and balance the budget too soon*. Instead you first give them all the tools they need for a good exercise regimen—*revenue*. Then you put them on a serious diet—*spending cuts*. The person through exercise—*revenue increase*—and diet—*spending cuts*—starts to lose weight—*shrinks the deficit and the size of government*. Instead of getting hurt by losing weight overnight—*screwing the economy by cutting too soon*—the person accepts the fact it might take a year or two to lose the weight—*the shit takes time*.

This means priorities have to be put in order. You can't put deficit reduction first on the list and put economic growth second because a weak economy makes it impossible to get the deficit under control. It's also a myth, as I just said, to grow the economy by shrinking the deficit. So what do you do? You start with the economy first. Putting people back to work has to be tops on the list. The faster these people start getting back to work, the stronger the economy will become. It might even take (gasp) some targeted spending. The American people are worth investing in. Instead of using taxpayer money to nation build overseas, use those same dollars to nation build right here at home. It's money well spent and it's a return on your dollar that you can actually see.

Our economic recovery is wobbly and sluggish, but it's a recovery nonetheless. Most economist agree that a small infusion of cash here and there would definitely help. Infrastructure spending is one of the best examples. It has always been popular with both parties because it's so practical. It creates jobs and there's a huge number of roads and bridges across the country that need to be repaired as soon as possible. This type of spending can nudge the economy to grow a bit faster.

Now that the economy is the number one priority for the short term—2 or 3 more years—you pay for the short term investment with long term deficit reduction. It should be a plan that is carefully implemented about two or three years from now. That might sound too slow but the fact is deficits are going to be huge over the next few years. There's just no getting around that.

Even Paul Ryan's budget reflects these facts. Despite shitting on everybody who's not rich and cutting everything except Donald Trump's hair, his budget sill adds several trillion in debt and does not forecast a balanced budget for almost 30 years. If a trillion dollar deficit was to be cut by say…700 billion over the next two years, you would not only still have a deficit but you would knock several million people out of the workforce. I know libertarians might not believe this but it's an economic fact. The key is long term deficit reduction over the next several years.

Every deficit commission and most economist, politicians, pundits, etc...have embraced a set number of 4 trillion dollars. Everyone sees 4 trillion as the magic number for deficit reduction. If Congress can find a way to reduce the deficit by 4 trillion over the next decade then this should put us all on the path to fiscal sanity. Four trillion seems to be that needed and reachable number.

If you followed the debt ceiling debate there was mass confusion as to how to reach 4 trillion dollars in deficit reduction over the next decade. Every expert known to man gave an opinion. Republicans wanted to cut 5 trillion dollars but use a trillion of that to pay for another round of tax cuts for the rich, and Democrats wanted to just raise taxes on the rich because they finally found something popular with the public to squawk about. This, of course, would justify giving Republicans everything else they demanded. It was a disgusting display of idiocy.

President Obama tried to get John "Bullshit" Boehner behind closed doors for a "Grand Bargain". They reached a compromise that in any normal frame of mind Republicans would love. Of course, Republicans are never in a normal frame of mind when their guy is not in the White House so they went into predictable hysteria.

The thought of giving Obama a victory was like some guy thinking about his wife having sex with the milkman after which she lets the lactose Don Juan sit in his easy chair while wearing his (the husband's) robe. It was taboo, and Republicans were repulsed. It was a compromise, and that was bullshit. That would make Obama look like a moderate with a fiscal backbone. It's bad enough he's killed a shitload of terrorists, now he looks like the voice of reason. Nope, not having it. This is a nightmare.

What made the situation even more grotesque is listening to the talking heads justify the intense Mexican standoff between the president and Republicans by saying how complicated this matter was. Four trillion dollars was no easy number to reach, and there was no easy answers, blah, blah.

Actually it's not quite as complicated as they made out. It's just a political risk. That's what it boils down to. The irony is we hate for our politicians to lie, but we vote against them when they tell us the truth if it doesn't coincide with what we want to hear. When a real deficit reduction plan does come before the nation, it won't be liked either. That's a fact. In fact, there has never been a deficit reduction plan that was popular. If it was, it didn't really do much of shit except produce a smoke screen. Bill Clinton hiked taxes and it was not a pretty sight, but the country appreciated the results. The results are what helped them forgive Clinton and re-elect him. The results are what mattered.

It's going to take some real supersized testicles but it needs to be done and the country will appreciate the results. So what's the first ugly, unpopular step? It's a blast from the past that starts with the Bush tax cuts. People everywhere, including myself, have complained that the Bush tax cuts have only benefited the rich. If that's the case then it should not be an Earth shattering event to let all the Bush tax cuts expire. To just let them expire on the rich is popular, but it won't really put a dent in the deficit. It's also not a good idea to do this now. Nothing should risk hurting the recovery, no matter how slim the odds are that it would.

However, in two or three years—*maximum*—the economy will be ready to implement this. All this means is that people would pay at the same tax rates they paid in the 90's when the economy was booming. The Bush tax cuts did absolutely nothing to stimulate the economy. Just like all those "silly experts" told Bush, the tax cuts were pretty damn "silly". They created huge deficits and the economy grew at a slow sluggish pace while interest rates on the debt created jobs...in other countries. But we had tax cuts...for the rich!!!

So, it's a no-brainer. If the tax cuts were really just for the rich and the facts are this obvious then it's time to let them expire. Now it's good politics to just let taxes go up on the rich. In fact, it's pretty understandable. The middle class and the poor have been getting screwed for a while, so why not show some favoritism? The thing is this type of policy might have a populist tone but it's going to hurt the middle class and the poor in the long run. The reason for this is simple. The smaller the tax hikes, the bigger the spending cuts are going to be. Those spending cuts are going to be a direct hit on the middle class and the poor. The deficit has to be brought under control. It's going to be painful so pick your poison. It's either going to be the Paul "Asshole" Ryan method which says everybody suffers except the rich or it's going to be the Clinton method. A combination of tax hikes and spending cuts.

Clinton's method is a proven success. Programs for the

poor and middle class were protected for the most part and the economy boomed at the same time. Ryan's method looks like something from an Ed Sullivan re-run featuring Barry Goldwater and Leave it to Beaver's school of economics.

Here's the kicker. Just letting the Bush tax cuts expire would reduce the deficit by 3.3 trillion dollars over the next decade. Just like that we are 82 percent closer to the magic 4 trillion mark. It's not that complicated.

Republicans and Democrats know this. The Bush tax cuts are what wiped out Clinton's surplus and blew holes in the deficit. Since that's the case let's make that our starting point for reducing the deficit. Democrats have rightly complained that the tax cuts were for the rich and didn't stimulate the economy. Then now is the time to show it. If these tax cuts didn't give the middle class and the poor an incentive to spend more after nine years then they shouldn't be all that traumatizing to let them expire.

That 3.3 trillion dollars of revenue would take a lot of pressure off of the economy by keeping Republicans from putting a hatchet to it. That still leaves 700 billion in cuts that they agree on. Before we get to the cuts, there is some other cost-saving measures as well. The tax code is filled with loopholes that favor the filthy rich. There's an estimated 12 trillion dollars over the next decade—in loopholes. These loopholes also have political risks since many of these same lobbyist who pushed for such loopholes are lining the pockets of the politicians that were pressured to put them there.

So, let's make it easy and realistic. Of the 12 *trillion* dollars in loopholes, let's close about 300 *billion* of them. Remember that dumbass super committee that was supposed to reduce the deficit by 1.2 trillion dollars over the next decade but they couldn't agree on what to eat for lunch much less how to cut spending?

This group of jerks, I mean Democrats and Republicans, seemed to agree on about 300 billion in tax hikes by closing loopholes.

So, if we add that to the 3.3 trillion dollars we already have then we have just reduced the deficit by 3.6 trillion. So we are now looking at another 400 billion to get to our magic number. Both sides have identified close to 1 trillion in cuts that they both agree on. So, let's make Republicans happy. Let's go ahead and find another 600 *billion* in spending cuts over the next decade. That's a whole lot smaller than the 5 *trillion* in cuts alone that Republicans want.

So, just like that we are over our magic number and we haven't even touched the sacred cows of both parties yet. These cows include defense spending (Republicans), Medicare and Social Security (Democrats). This doesn't mean we don't have to. It means we can simply tweak them and make a few unpopular adjustments instead of dismantling them the way Republicans want to.

Now, before we get into entitlements, we have seen the two options before us. We have the Clinton option and we have the Paul Ryan option. The only other option is the Obama option.

During the debt ceiling debate, President Obama and House Speaker, John Boehner went behind closed doors and came up with a "Grand Bargain". It was a combination of spending cuts and tax hikes, we think. The fact is we just don't know a whole lot about the grand bargain other than the fact that Obama was willing to cut Medicare and Social Security in exchange for tax hikes on the rich.

Various sources, including the president, said the deal involved 1.2 trillion dollars in tax hikes and 2.6 trillion in spending cuts. A grand total of 3.8 trillion in deficit reduction. The House Speaker has not denied these numbers.

Because I don't know the details (and no one else does either), one can only speculate how these spending cuts would be spread around. The fact is the cuts would be deep. Many of you reading this book might favor Obama's approach. This approach worries me because of the hit many programs for the poor and the middle class would take. I can tell you this though. I like Obama's approach a whole lot more than I like Paul Ryan's. Ryan's plan cuts 5 trillion dollars, but only reduces the deficit by 4 trillion because of huge *tax cuts* for the rich. Obama's approach cuts <u>half</u> of what Ryan's budget does (2.6 trillion) but reduces the deficit by almost 4 trillion dollars because of a trillion in *tax hikes* on the rich.

If Obama would have offered the details of this approach, it would have been received better by the public than Ryan's, but liberals would have still went a little nuts because he did seem to touch up entitlements pretty good.

Nevertheless, it still was better than turning Medicare into a voucher program just so that the rich could get some more tax breaks. Yeah, I think I would take the Obama plan over Ryan's plan any day.

So, we have a few ideas here. We can let all the Bush tax cuts expire to hit the magic number. This would involve 85 percent tax hikes, and 15 percent in cuts. It's much more simple and it makes sense. The economy boomed and the budget was balanced four straight years with those same tax rates.

I think these tax cuts should expire in two parts. Let the ones for the rich expire at the end of this year. The rest should be extended until about 2015. The reason for this is obvious. The economy will be much stronger and several million more people will be in the workforce. The unemployment rate should be at a much more reasonable level, around 6.5 percent, maybe lower, if the economy hits its stride and lawmakers quit neglecting it.

This means wages would be starting to increase again. As wages increase, the invisible tax break could be phased out slowly over a two year span. A tax hike at this stage of the game would sort of be a slap in the face to the middle class because middle class wages remain flat. The people who have suffered the most don't need to be feeling any type of pinch right now and for at least the next few years. No matter how small.

Like I said earlier, it was already a chicken shit tax cut for the middle class and the poor, so that bullshit tax cut should not be a tradeoff that justifies cutting into programs that benefit them the most. I don't believe this is a good trade off at all.

Instead, phase it out while wages are increasing so that it won't be painful or just let the damn things expire.

That's one option. The second option is to hike taxes on the rich and cut spending a lot. Obama is willing to give Republicans three dollars in spending cuts to every dollar in tax hikes. That's unheard of for a big deficit reduction package. Reagan would have done cartwheels to get a deal like that.

Again, it's hard to really make a fair judgment on this one. As of right now, it seems to me that it would take more than just tax hikes on the rich to spare the economy and entitlements. However, Obama's budget did make some serious cuts to discretionary spending.

Going back to 1962, domestic discretionary spending has hovered around 3.3 percent of GDP. Since Obama has been in office it ended up peaking at around 4 percent of GDP. In the president's budget however, that spending would fall to around 2.2 percent of GDP. As columnist David Brooks noted, "that is lower than anything Reagan achieved."

I would rather see discretionary spending cut to a more modest level of around 2.8 percent of the GDP. Things like education should not have to be put under this type of knife just because the tax code is rigged.

Nevertheless, if just taxing the rich can get you there

with sensible cuts then I am all for it. It just makes things a whole lot more complicated, and when things become complicated in Washington they become impossible. Then we have our last option. Paul Ryan's plan. Now Ryan's plan is supposed to be about reducing the deficit, in fact, I have been being nice when I say that his savage cuts reduce the deficit by 4 trillion dollars. Actually, we don't know for sure if Ryan's plan really reduces the deficit or not. For now, let's just say it does. It slams the middle class and the poor. In fact, it throws those two groups under a bus. This should not even be an option, but it is and not a very good one at that.

The only common theme in all of them is that tax reform is a must and that entitlements have to be touched.

I feel like Medicare only has to be tweaked. A bump in the payroll tax, a bump in premiums for very wealthy seniors and maybe a slight increase in deductibles. It won't take much to get Medicare sustainable for another fifty or sixty years.

Ryan's plan turns the program into a voucher system. This is utterly stupid. Maybe my method might need one or two dislikeable tweaks at the most, and that's a wrap. Medicare is okay. Even the (Conservative) Heritage Foundation admitted that an increase in the payroll tax would solve the problem. They said they don't support such a method but it would solve the problem. I added the payroll tax jump idea with a few other slight (but dislikable) tweaks. That should do it.

The thing is, whatever approach that's taken to deficit

reduction should not be driven by ideology. It should be driven by facts, data, and proven methods of success. If both sides don't dislike it then nine times out of ten it didn't do anything. It's going to have to be balanced and it's going to have to have a liberal imprint as well as a conservative imprint.

So we see that spending cuts alone and spending cuts right now do not benefit the economy as a whole. The only group who goes untouched by the cuts are the rich. Their reward for watching everybody else suffer is more tax breaks. This method is reckless and dangerous. If we are going to accept a deficit reduction plan that we hate let's at least be faced with one that's practical and one that actually benefits the people who are going to be hit hardest by such a plan. A plan that is beneficial to the middle class and the poor will make the rich a lot more richer. A plan like Ryan's gives the rich are more tax breaks they don't need but after that free handout we all find ourselves back to square one.

People say Paul Ryan's plan might suck, but at least it's courageous. Please explain to me what is so courageous about putting together a budget that shits on the same people who haven't supported you or your party in decades, but caters to the ones who fund your campaign? What in the name of common sense is so courageous about a budget that steps on the people who do not have the power and clout on Capitol Hill to defend themselves?

If that's courage then we should go ahead and award the medal of bravery to Ted Nugent for courageously squeezing his washed up country singing ass into those

Wrangler jeans that haven't fit right in 20 years.

A courageous budget would have been one that spits in the face of his conservative base with *needed* tax increases, while telling liberals to screw off by reforming entitlements. That would have been a bit more courageous instead of this bullshit ideology. The conservative ideology no longer lines up with fact. The sad part is this clown knows it and he knows it's bullshit, but it stirs his base. Conservatives wouldn't care what he has in his budget as long as it's opposite of Obama's.

Obama seems more interested in getting the economy back on track. Conservatives go the opposite route. They say screw the economy. Just cut, cut, cut. It's ironic that these cuts, at this moment, would slow economic growth at a time when it's desperately needed.

I am not trying to imply that Republicans would want to sabotage the economy just to beat Obama, but it does make some cock an eyebrow. Think about it. They didn't want to negotiate a stimulus plan which looks a lot like a Republican spending bill. They cried out against the auto bailouts, but said nothing when Bush started the program. It's now a proven fact that the bailouts worked, so they claim it was still wrong for government to intervene. They flashed all the way outside the reality zone during the debt ceiling debate and begged voters to believe that if the debt ceiling was not raised everything would be okay. Every economist and sane individual who knows how to add refuted those claims. Even the U.S. credit rating was downgraded for the first time. After realizing voters were not buying into their delusions, Republicans succumbed to public pressure and raised the debt ceiling. That was the only reason they raised it. Public pressure was the only reason they extended the middle class payroll tax cut and unemployment benefits at the start of this year. It's a bit suspicious that now at a time when the economy desperately needs money that conservatives cry out for spending cuts that they themselves never had the courage to enact when they had the power to do so.

Okay, I *am* trying to imply that Republicans are sabotaging the economy for the sake of winning an election. If they are not, it's the most coincidental sequence of events known to mankind. It's one of those situations where your wife's sister comes in your house drunk while you're sound asleep. Your wife is at work, so the sister gets naked, stumbles in the bedroom, and falls (accidentally) on top of the sound asleep unsuspecting husband who never moves. The wife comes home and sees her naked husband and sister both sound asleep on top of each other at which time you jump up and reassure her that it's not what it looks like. It was all just a big coincidence, that you're really just an innocent, faithful husband.

If that scenario can be believed, then I suppose it's only reasonable to assume that Republicans are not actually trying to slow the economic recovery to regain power. It's simply a case of mistaken identity.

All this could be happening because they are actually stupid. Really stupid. Like Lindsey Lohan in a shopping mall stupid. This could almost be possible except for the whole Paul Ryan guy. This guy studied economics. He knows better. He knows his own budget is not worth spending. It's social engineering that reflects a warped, perverted, and foolish world view. It's his base. Conservatives. This is what they want. Not a good budget. A good dog fight with the president and he's obliged. He stands up to the president...with bullshit, but he stands up to the president and that's what counts.

That's what these spending cuts are all about. They're so bad that Republicans only preach them when they are not in power and don't have to worry about facing the disastrous consequences when implemented. The ones who would implement this shit follow Paul's lead.

Conservatives are following him lock step. Where he heads they will go. To the nuthouse that is.

6 | DEREGULATION AND THE MORONS WHO PUSH FOR IT

Now the last component of this sophisticated ideology is deregulation. Explaining this method along with its history can become extremely boring. So for the sake of your own sanity, I will just go ahead and make this as quick as possible. If you feel it's too vague, just complain to me and I will go ahead and base my next book on this topic.

For now, here's the gist of it. As I already mentioned before, the country was experiencing economic meltdowns on a pretty regular basis. Not recessions, but total economic collapses. This was due in main part to a flawed banking system. Other factors would contribute to the catastrophes once the meltdowns started. This sort of unsupervised banking system was leaving the country vulnerable to any type of unforeseen circumstance that came along.

As time when on, government saw it necessary to put certain regulations in place to protect the economy. What many conservatives don't realize is that many banks and institutions begged the government to put certain regulations in place. It wasn't the idea of a bunch of socialistic liberals. Businesses and banks were tired of failing because of chronic meltdowns. The government also realized that many megabanks and businesses were using certain tactics that led to panics. Bank runs at the drop of a hat killed a lot of banks and wreaked economic havoc throughout the private sector as a result. A lot of band aids were put in place, but none were actually safe guarding the country as well as needed.

That all changed in the 1930's. The Great Depression (and the idiotic reaction of Hoover) led to universal anger and frustration. The American people were suffering and they were pissed. Then of course, came "The New Deal". The objective was simple. Put regulations in place that prevent another depression. Put regulations in place that are bold and sweeping. Government must supervise the market in order to protect everyday citizens from suffering for the sins of a few bankers who let greed get the best of them.

The Security Exchange Commission, along with a number of other reforms, were put into place. Conservatives decried this as socialism. The mass majority of Americans said thank you. After the Roosevelt-Truman era, Eisenhower would claim the White House and he would not lay a finger on the New Deal. When Nixon came into power after the J.F.K.-L.B.J. era, he too would not lay a finger on the New Deal.

After an economy that boomed in the 1960's started to stall, it was clear economic hardships were ahead. The cause for the sloppy economy in the 1970's was an inflation crisis. Unemployment at one point got as high as nine percent in the 1970's. It was, however, a far cry from the unemployment rate that hit 25 percent in 1933. The country started to bounce back again only to tip back into recession in 1981. This time unemployment would peak at 10.8 percent. When inflation started to fall in the 80's, so did the unemployment rate. In fact, it fell rapidly.

These recessions in no way mirrored the Great Depression era. They didn't last half as long as a depression. The average recession lasted about two years since World War II. The unemployment rate never came close to anything resembling depression either. The contrast is pretty clear to see. Recessions happen, but they are whole lot different than depressions. The economic collapse felt during the Great Depression was a severe strain on the fabric of America that was too painful and dangerous to be repeated.

Since the New Deal was put in place that pain has not been repeated since. In fact, this is the longest streak the U.S. has ever experienced without succumbing to an all-out depression. The regulations worked and they didn't stop the U.S. from prospering. The economy still had record expansions along the way and strong job growth.

Then a new era would begin. Despite effective protection and stunning success from the New Deal era regulations, a new day would dawn. Thanks to a new asshole on the scene.

Alan Greenspan would usher in a new era of stupidity. Like I said earlier, this guy has a pretty sensational story, but I will resist the temptation to elaborate too much on what a world class penis face he is. What's relevant at the moment is that Greenspan would be appointed to lead the Federal Reserve in 1987. Ronald Reagan would get rid of the guy who saved his presidency. Paul Volker is one of the most underrated heroes of the 1980's. While Reagan was basking in the glow of an economic renaissance, it was Volker steering the ship. The economy sucked, unemployment was sky high, and Ronald Reagan was on the verge of being a one term president. Those stupid tax cuts weren't paying for themselves either. The Federal Reserve's tight money policy proved to be on point. Inflation began to freefall and so did the unemployment rate. Reagan happily went behind closed doors and told Tip O'Neil—the House Speaker—well, now that shit is falling into place let's go ahead and take away about 132 billion dollars of those stupid ass tax breaks I gave out. At least that's what it seems he said, since he did exactly that.

So, how did Reagan reward Paul Volker? He replaced him with a real economic guru named Alan Greenspan. It was a natural choice. Greenspan already proved his worth to the president when he helped him scam the middle class out of 1.69 trillion. He was also everything a president could want in a colleague. A real live ass sucker. That's an underrated quality in politics.[1]

Everyone from Greenspan's biographer, Jerome Tuccile to officials like Martin Anderson, talk about Greenspan's skill of being with the right people, to being in the right place inside of the White House. Paul Volker was a prude who was more interested in doing his job, and doing it well. Greenspan meanwhile, had his head so far up the asses of so many people around the Capitol that if any would have burped his eyeglasses might have come flying out of the person's mouth.[1]

Greenspan would be appointed in 1987, and it wasn't because of his economic skill either. His past predictions were always wrong and he seemed to be tracking the economy, just not the one here in the U.S. This was made evident during the Senate nomination process that he was forced to endure. A senator from Wisconsin named William Proxmire hammered Greenspan's record from his days as Ford's counsel of economic advisors.[1]

In one of the most memorable exchanges, Greenspan was determine to correct the Senator and clear up a misunderstanding concerning one of his predictions. The Senator *maliciously* tried to accuse Greenspan of predicting a T-bill rate of 4.4 percent for 1978. The rate was actually 9.8 percent. He also slammed him for allegedly predicting that the consumer price index would rise 4.5 percent when it actually rose 9.5 percent. Boy, that Senator Proxmire is ruthless, huh? I mean, only a complete moron could get those predictions wrong like that, right?[1]

Greenspan would bravely declare: "That is not my recollection of the way those forecasts went."[1]

Proxmire ended up reading all the predictions like a list of felony charges.

Greenspan now realizing for the first time apparently, that his rap sheet was in front of Proxmire finally admitted: "Well, if they're written down, those are the numbers."[1]

Despite the fact it was confirmed at a Senate hearing that Alan Greenspan is a full blown idiot and moron, he would be sworn in as the Fed Chief on August 11, 1987. It would lead to an era that called for not only deregulation, but an economy that would produce severe bubbles along the way. It would usher in an era of Wall St. excess and Main St. paying the price.[1]

The Federal Reserve has a lot of different functions. Some of the main ones are: enforcing banking regulations to maintain and cause currency to conform to certain standards, and the biggest—regulating supply of money.[1]

Regulating the money supply is supposed to keep the economy growing at a healthy pace. Mostly by limiting inflation and preventing recession. So, let's say there is too much buying and inflation. The Fed will contract money, basically pulling money out of the economy to keep inflation in check. But if there's not enough money in the economy this could cause a recession so the Fed loosens credit and adds to the money supply.[1]

The power and scope of the Fed cannot be understated. It can not only create money but it can inject it into the system. The Fed can take an already productive economy and through the right methods turn it into a powerhouse. But if it allows the whole economy to be turned into an unsupervised circus, then plowing new money into such a playhouse becomes destructive. To keep injecting cash into the hands of a bunch of morons who lose it faster than Brittany Spears lost her hair just makes the whole situation worse. Feeding this circus is what Alan Greenspan specialized in.[1]

Greenspan fought tooth and nail against regulating certain forms of derivatives.[1]

He fought the regulation despite seeing the damage done firsthand by what happens when they're not policed properly.[1]

Just a few months after taking office, there was the Stock Market Corrections of 1987. Among other things one of the main culprits of the crash was portfolio insurance derivatives. In fact, these instruments were responsible for at least five disasters throughout the 1990's. One of the scariest was when long term management imploded in '98. It almost swamped the global economy in the process. Greenspan always handled these disasters in the same way. He would slash the federal funds rate and flood the economy with a lot of money.[1]

From May of 1989 to July of 1991, he slashed the federal funds rate by 36 percent. He would cut rates by another whopping 44 percent by the fall of 1992. He kept the rates at extremely low levels for over a year straight. He finally raised rates again in February of 1994. It was the first time in five years.[1]

Now you might be asking, what's the big deal? So what if he slashed these rates? Slashing rates sound like a good thing, right? Well, here's the problem. He was slashing fund rates. This affects rates on anything and everything. When this clown slashed these rates it caused CD's, T-bills, commercial bonds, savings accounts, etc...to drop as well. Then here comes all the baby boomers who are getting ready to retire. All these people have money tied up in CD's, and a variety of investments that were drawing interest to give them a nice sized nest egg for when they retire. Well, come to find out these investments are losing yields. In fact, these investments were losing yields for five straight years.[1]

So, where was that money going? Wall St. was taking five years of free money and investing in all types of nice stock. This forced baby boomers and others to rush into the equity markets. If not, they were going to get stuck with declining yields on what was supposed to be safe investments. Either get into riskier investments or lose out was the ultimatum. Because of this a bubble was already forming in 1994. The remedy for this oncoming disaster is to either raise rates or increase the margin requirements. So, he hikes the rate by one half of a percentage point. He then announced in August of 1994, the bubble is popped thanks to the courageous rate hike of one half of a percentage point.[1]

After one small rate hike in 1995, he went back to slashing fund rates like he lost his mind. The money was flooding through the stock market. Then in 1996, it seemed (even according to him) that asset values had become over inflated. Everybody started to get a little spooked. But Greenspan would save the day. He chopped rates and chopped them some more. He would chop so much that over a three year span the money supply expanded by over one and a half trillion dollars. While Wall St. was loving all the money falling from the sky, a major bubble was brewing underneath the service.[1]

While that bubble was being fed during that span from 1996 to 1999, another disaster was taking place. Long term capital management went up in smoke in 1998. Their dickhead managers decided to leverage themselves a few hundred times over. This way they could gamble on all those risky derivatives. Well, when the idiots caused complete chaos, it was Greenspan who came to the rescue. He helped orchestrate a bailout, because it was a "systematic risk" for the fund to fail. This was unheard of. The Fed bailing out LTCM was the start of a trend. It sent a clear message. The days of Herbert Hoover are back. If Wall St. gets in a bind the Fed will save your ass, by any means necessary. So, go ahead and have a blast.[1]

And a blast they had. All that over inflated stock led to the bubble finally bursting in 2000. More than 5 trillion dollars in wealth had been utterly destroyed. He, of course, cut rates some more. The tech bubble busted and it spilled over into Main St. in the form of a two year recession. Greenspan meanwhile would try to make investors feel better by slashing interest eleven consecutive times. Interest rates would fall to 1 percent. This artificial money would set the stage for the housing market collapse.[1]

While this was taking place, Greenspan would pull of one of the slickest crimes in U.S. history. If you thought the Social Security scam was something, this is going to really impress you. One of the ironic parts of the whole situation is that he's the Fed Chief. His job is to oversee all banking activity. He's the sheriff in town. Instead of working hard to enforce his regulatory power he worked hard at stripping himself of all authority.[1]

Before Greenspan, the Fed had the power to enforce margin requirements. It had the ability to restrict derivative trades and it was able to stop unlawful mergers. Greenspan weakened the Fed greatly. Thanks to him, the only thing the Fed was enforcing was the ability to give shitloads of money to banks and what janitor should work the night shift at the Central Bank.[1]

The huge step to neutering the Fed was destroying the Glass-Steagall Act. This act was one of the many reforms passed during the New Deal era.[1]

The law barred insurance companies, investment banks, and commercial banks from merging. The law's main focus was to stop the merger of a single mega-company that would create potential conflicts of interest. It also was designed to safeguard us from the "too big to fail" banks and institutions. These very same types of institutions are what needed the bailouts of 2008 and tied the hands of the government.[1]

In 1998, Sandy Weill, the Chairman of Citibank, orchestrated the merger of his bank with *two* other huge financial institutions. Travelers which was an investment banking giant, and Salomon Smith Barney. Now this whole merger was illegal. Glass-Steagall was still a law at this time and this merger spit right in the face of it.[1]

The merger, however was backed by all the right people. Everyone from the President, to his Treasury Secretary, to Alan Greenspan got behind it. Greenspan approved the deal even though it was illegal. He used a provision in the Bank Holding Company Act that allowed the merger to go through...*temporarily*. The act basically gave Citigroup up to five years to divorce itself from its newly married partners.[1]

Now the next move is the real kicker because it really shows you the audacity of Greenspan.[1]

After circumventing Congress to illegally merge these firms and use a flimsy loophole to bide him some time, he then uses his own illegal act to put Congress over a barrel.[1]

In February 1999, he tells them: "Without congressional action to update our laws the market will force AD HOC administration responses that lead to inefficiencies and inconsistencies, expansion of the federal safety net, and potentially increased risk exposure to the federal deposit insurance funds."[1]

Translation:
If you guys don't get off your sorry asses and repeal this law, the market is going to throw up all over the place, people everywhere are going to be forced to live on welfare, and we're going to go bankrupt while the sky comes crashing down on top of everyone in this room.

Greenspan had circumvented Congress and told them in so many words that it was too late. Do the deal or die. Congress caved, and thus the era of real deregulation had only begun.[1]

The repeal of Glass-Steagall would open the door to a new law. The Gramm-Leach-Bliley Act would lead to a new legalized deal post factum.[1]

In 2000, the Commodity Futures Modernization Act was passed. Greenspan pushed hard for this law which completely deregulated the derivatives market. The law not only prevented the federal government from regulating everything from collateralized debt obligations and credit default swaps, it even stopped states from regulating them. Despite the disasters and meltdowns of the 90's caused by derivatives, Greenspan deregulated them completely. The funny part is most rational people try to give him a rational explanation that doesn't make it look like he did it to feed the greed of a few while throwing caution to the wind with everyone else. That might not have been his intention but that's exactly what he did.[1]

Every piece of deregulation and rate cutting not only was a tactic to cater to Wall St., but it was the opening salvos for the economic collapse of 2008. Greenspan was putting all the pieces in place.

In 2004, Greenspan started encouraging homeowners that adjustable rate mortgages were safer and more attractive than fixed rate mortgages. In a speech to the Credit Union National Association Governmental Affairs Conference in February 2004, he drones on about this very topic. He said, "Indeed, recent research within the Federal Reserve suggests that many homeowners might have saved tens of thousands of dollars had they held adjustable rate mortgages rather than fixed rate mortgages during the past decade." Later on he says: "American consumers might benefit if lenders provided greater mortgage product alternatives to the traditional fixed rate mortgages." Then not long after he says: "The traditional fixed rate mortgage may be an expensive method of financing a home."[1]

After convincing homeowners to go with adjustable rates, Greenspan turned right around and raised rates for 17 straight months. He quadrupled rates from 1 percent to 4.5 percent. He basically convinced people to give up traditional fixed rates and suckered them to go with adjustable rates. Then he jacked rates sky high causing homeowners to pay a shitload of more money to their lenders.[1]

Couple that with his mad scramble to deregulate everything. His deregulation scored a direct hit on the housing bubble. The most devastating aspect of his deregulation methods was the derivatives market.

Bankers were taking certain derivatives and using them to chop shop for mortgage debt. They would take bad loans and dress them all up as AAA rated investments and dump the shit off on a secondary market. This would be passed off as securities and it was big money. These top notch investments would be sold to everyone from pension funds to unions, and insurance companies. Wall St. made billions off these toxic mortgages.[1]

Alan Greenspan bragged about today's "technological

advances" that lenders were taking advantage of. This new technology was "extending credit to a broader spectrum of consumers."[1]

Translation:
We got shit in place that allows us to manipulate credit ratings so that we can lend money to people with no credit, job or proof of existence, and lenders can sell these fools off on someone else in the form of a Grade A investment.

From 2003 to 2005, America had an outstanding mortgage debt that grew by 3.7 trillion dollars. In just two years, America had borrowed almost as much as it had the previous 200 years combined. The surge in lending and home buying thanks to a Ponzi scheme on Wall St. was creating a bubble even larger than the one that burst in 2000.[1]

This deregulated Wall St. would have a blast and Greenspan would give them all the money they needed to do so.

Then of course, the bubble burst. The housing market collapsed. It was the worst economic meltdown in decades. Alan Greenspan gave conservatives all the deregulation they could ever want, and the hilarious part is they probably didn't even know it. You know why? Because the only people who benefit from the doctrine of deregulation is the millionaires running casinos on Wall St. Once they get adult supervision put on them, they scream "big government" from the rooftops. The big government is invading the private sector. Conservatives on Main St.

who have no idea what the details are of such a fight, hear their own elected leaders echo the battle cry of Wall St. and follow suit.[1]

Most senseless and moronic regulations that conservatives know about are the ones that smack them hard on a local level. Government can fine you for grass not being cut, too many cars in the driveway, where you can fish, this type of bullshit can drive somebody insane. Attention Conservatives: That's not what we're talking about! When the New Deal era regulations started being peeled away by Greenspan and his bosses in the White House, it left the country vulnerable to the same type of shady practices that caused the crash of 1929. Only this time, "technology" was more advanced.

So the economy is bigger now and the consequences could be even more dangerous.

Deregulation in the 1800's was not working so it led to more and more regulations until the Great Depression. Then of course, came the New Deal. Coincidentally, we haven't had a depression since the New Deal. Another coincidence is we have the worst economic catastrophe since the depression and it comes on the heels of a deregulating bonanza by Greenspan and Company. It's no coincidence though. The deregulation methods that Greenspan pushed for is what led to the collapse of the housing market.

So, conservatives believe in fairy tales concerning tax cuts. They are on a crusade for spending cuts that don't make sense, and deregulation is the key to a prospering economy even though a deregulated economy always blows up in everybody's face. This is the conservative economic ideology. It's one that doesn't coincide with reality. The irony is that they cry and whine about wanting their country back. Well, if they are referring to the 40's, 50's and 1960's then they better take a close look at what they're asking for.

During those golden years, the rich were paying more in taxes, spending was increasing on an expanding safety net, and Wall St. was regulated. Of course, these little details are overlooked. You see, what they remember is the U.S. not saddled with debt. Let's give a shout to Reagan on that one. They remember an economy that seemed to be expanding. They didn't have to concern themselves with doctrine of regulation, because anybody with any sense wasn't going to touch the New Deal. Of course they became desperate for power, so an outcast like Barry Goldwater suddenly seems sensible.

But, why did they fall in line with such a warped economic ideology? Probably because it relates to their social views. It's an ideology that discriminates against the poor. Helping the poor is supposed to give them an incentive to be poor, and you don't want to do that. You don't want poor people to be satisfied with their social condition. This is not reality. It's an excuse to justify snubbing the poor. The poor are poor because they're lazy. They lack the ambition of rich people. That's why rich people are rich and poor people are poor.

This dime store logic doesn't match up with "the rule". The "exception" to the rule is that some poor people might be crazy and lazy. Yet in general, most people not only want to get out of poverty but many work harder than rich people. Have you ever seen a poor person on a job site? They always stick out like a sore thumb. It's as if they are dying for the chance to show that they belong.

The conservative economic ideology preaches that these poor people will have their job and a chance at prosperity if the rich are taken care of first because the rich are the drivers of wealth. As I said before, this is a bunch of crap. Yet, this is their social view so they adopt it as practical economics no matter how many times it fails.

It's a social view that says lazy Black people are the reason for the housing market collapsed. The hard working taxpayers have to redistribute their money to welfare programs for the lazy minorities. Maybe that's the only reason they want traditional America back. Who knows? What we do know is that facts and data mean nothing to these people. Conservative politicians are bought off by Wall St. so they feed this bullshit to their conservative base who protest in the name of smaller government. The whole while they're doing the bidding of the very elitist that they claim to despise.

The very people who wiped out 40 percent of the world's wealth. The very people that are responsible for 8 million jobs being destroyed in less than two years.

Conservatives don't care though. All they care about is being in power. That's it. The facts don't mean shit. It's their country and they want it back. Their economic ideology is a testament to this. If they adjust it to line up with reality they will be dishonoring the tradition of their own party. That would make them reasonable. It would make them flexible. Damn...that would make them almost...liberal!!! Hell no, ain't happening. That would be like Michelle Bachmann admitting that gay people are human beings too. That's way too over the top.

No, the best thing to do is just double down on an ideology that makes no sense. After all, isn't that how Reagan won the White House? Who gives a shit what he did after he got there. He won. And even if he didn't, who cares? He still won. This ideology is a winner even if it doesn't work.

It reflects the way things are supposed to be. It reflects hard work and small government. It reflects success rewarded and laziness punished.

At least, that's what they want it to reflect. It actually reflects discrimination. It reflects a government that's bought off by Wall St. so it turns a blind eye to the people that need it most.

It reflects a group of people who are shallow and self-centered. Their narcissism is nauseating and their self-pity for not being recognized as the most patriotic people since the founding fathers is grotesque. Their economic ideology is how they feel. They want it to go back to the good old days when they were the focal part of the country.

That's how they explain tax cuts for people who don't need them. That's how they explain spending cuts that make no sense. That's how they explain deregulation as some type of silver bullet to cure the economy. In their minds these ideas stand on principle. Who needs facts? Facts are confusing and simply muddy the waters.

Facts can be a hindrance to power, so facts can be brushed to the side according to conservatives. It's not about facts, it's about *power*.

7 | THE ENGINE THAT MAKES THE WHOLE CAR RUN

In 1988, Ronald Reagan gave his reasons why he broke his campaign pledge concerning the budget. You see, Reagan didn't break his promise to balance the budget because of a spending spree that ran up record deficits. He broke his promise because of something called "The Iron Triangle". Congress, special interest...and the media.

The first two reasons are understandable. Special interest and Congress are pretty much bedfellows on Capitol Hill. The last one is a bit odd. Somehow the media prevented Reagan from submitting Congress a balanced budget. Damn that Dan Rather! He's always standing in the way of progress. Why couldn't he just let President Reagan balance the budget just once, please?!

This is nothing new or old with conservatives. They are really, really sensitive about the media. It's not necessarily because the media disagrees with them. It's when the media does not just up and kiss their asses that they (conservatives) get really peeved. If the media doesn't do backflips in support of their idea, speeches, etc…they go nuts and claim the 'liberal media' is out to get them. They go right back into Joe McCarthy mode.

Richard Nixon once whined, "You won't have Nixon to kick around anymore."

Today, you see it more than ever. Conservatives just hate, hate, hate when the media refuses to glorify them.

Sarah Palin—a huge media hog—feels unfairly attacked by the liberal media. She claims the media is always setting her up with "gotcha" questions. Ah yes, that tricky liberal media is who lured her into that trap about Paul Revere. It all makes sense now. According to Palin's logic, the media must have known that she didn't have a clue concerning basic fourth grade history and waited to pounce on her the moment she distorted such well known facts. Ooh…that liberal media.

Even the most unbiased media outlets have a hard time not chuckling at Palin's obvious lack of intellect. This of course means she is being attacked. How dare the media expose an attention-craving junkie. So what if she begs to be in the limelight because the extra publicity helps her sell books. That doesn't mean she deserves the scrutiny that comes with such attention, right?

Give me a break, anyone who craves such attention and makes the ridiculous claims that this woman makes is going to be subjected to the same microscope. The reason she does not step back from such attention is because she enjoys the money and fame that comes with it. She's not seriously trying to help the 50 million living in poverty or help solve the country's problems. She's trying to sell books and make money. She's good at it too. So, while her loyal following holds a sympathy fest on her behalf, she's laughing all the way to the bank. The so called liberal media has made her a ton of money. Yet, conservatives cry about her being unfairly targeted by these hostile outlets.

Even during the GOP presidential debates, attacking the media was popular. Newt "Moonshot" Gingrich gained his fame in the primaries by accusing Chris Wallace of asking gotcha questions. The crowd loved it and his poll numbers soared. Forget the fact that the question was a very sincere and relevant one. Newt diverted attention from the issue and made himself look like he was above such pettiness. The funny part is that as soon as Newt had to actually start debating the issues and not the gotcha questions is when he started looking like the typical moron that he is.

Conservatives have long felt handcuffed by the fact that the mainstream media is not too impressed with them. Now, in all fairness, the media says and does things that are not factual at times. We know this. The media will also blow things out of proportion. Anyone who has ever been in the media knows this. All this almost goes without saying.

Conservatives on the other hand, take their sensitivities

to a whole new level. The liberal media is attacking them whenever it doesn't fawn over their ideas. The reason for this is actually pretty clever. Conservatives ideas tend to be pretty warped and backwards. Their ideas don't really make sense to mainstream America many times so, it's obvious the mainstream media won't buy into it. So by attacking the media, it makes it look like their message is just being distorted and not accurately translated. It gives them a foil to distract from the facts.

Just look at the Donald Trump circus. The so called liberal media gave this clown more airtime than Nancy Grace covering "Tot Mom". He became a regular on CNN. The liberal media is what made his ridiculous "birther" claim seem like it just might be worth talking about. They actually had this buffoon on the same set as politicians and political pundits as if he was going to give some insightful input.

Yes, the "liberal media" made him money and boosted his ratings on The Apprentice.

Yes, the "liberal media" invited him on the air to bash the so called liberal president.

The fact is the media is so scared of being labeled liberal now that they make some of the crap conservatives come with look legitimate. CNN is a good example of this. The only ones who seem to actually come across as bluntly honest sometime is Anderson Cooper and Pierce Morgan. And they are some of the time restraining themselves from just coming out and saying alright folks, this is really just a bunch of bullshit and I can't take it anymore, arghh!!!

CNN always makes sure it has a few conservative talking heads along with a few liberal talking heads, at which point the host tries to act as an unbiased referee. The coverage can seem watered down at times because the facts are usually sugar coated and the debates cut short when they become too heated.

All the other networks are even worse. It's as if everyone is trying to walk on eggshells so that the right wing bullies don't label them liberal. Even many of your pundits and columnists act like they're trying to win friends by flexing their intellectual capacity to see both sides of the issue and find a happy medium.

What they don't realize is a happy medium in the minds of conservatives is bullshit. That's like a compromise. It's the liberal media trying to disguise the fact that they're right. So, not only does the columnist lie by trying to sugarcoat the facts, but he then still gets nowhere with conservatives who feel that if you don't agree with them on *everything*, you're a liberal who's trying to destroy the traditions of America.

This is a pretty good idea by conservatives. Both sides always recognized the need for the media, but conservatives have always been much better at claiming to be attacked. They really fire their base up and play the role of martyr very well.

The thing is, attacking the media will only get you so far. Using the media to manipulate people to further a radical agenda is where it's at. That's how you not only get your message out, but you distort it and spin it anyway you want. One man understood this as well as anybody out there. He had the know how to make it happen too.

Roger Ailes is a gifted manipulator, he can take a big bowl of horseshit and spin it into a delicious quesadilla stuffed with meat and vegetables.

Ailes is the brainchild behind Fox News. To truly understand Fox News you must understand Roger Ailes. Once you understand Roger Ailes then you see the conservative movement that relies on his direction and leadership. You gain firsthand knowledge of the insanity and greed that drives today's conservative movement and makes them seem like a legitimate force.

Roger Ailes is another one of those characters that has a long and sensational story but for the sake of getting to the point, here's just a brief glimpse of the nut job who really pulls the strings of the entire conservative movement.

Ailes was born in Ohio and is the son of a Taft Republican. This little piece of info is extremely relevant. Senator Robert Taft of Ohio was the lead clown in the GOP circus against expanding the New Deal. In the late 1930's, his push is what gave birth to the Taft-Hartley act. This law is what helped clip the wings, and diminish power of labor unions. So from an early age, it's clear Roger Ailes didn't fall from the tree.[4]

He would study radio and television in college and land his first job on the Mike Douglas show. His rapid rise on the show would propel him to executive producer at the young age of 25.[4]

It was backstage at the Mike Douglas show that Ailes would meet the man who would change his life forever. Roger Ailes would become the reason that Richard Nixon would win the White House and Richard Nixon would be the doorway for Ailes to become the most shrewd political operative of his generation.[4]

After letting Nixon know in very blunt terms that "the camera doesn't like you", Ailes would change Nixon's whole mindset concerning television and media.[4]

The son of a Taft Republican who felt the biased liberal media was not going to give his dirty underhanded candidate a fair shake would simply create his own staged media and "*make* Nixon the star of his own traveling roadshow—a series contrived of news-like events that the campaign paid to broadcast in local markets across the country" is how Tim Dickinson of Rolling Stone magazine put it.[4]

Ailes would go around the real media by creating his own.

It was rigged inside of actual theatres where hand-picked puppets would ask Nixon retarded, easy questions that "played to Nixon's talking points", as Tim Dickinson put it. The theatre would be packed with Nixon supporters. Ailes would later claim that they were "an applause machine, that's all that they are."[4] It was practically The Late Show with Richard Nixon.

Journalists and the press were not allowed on the set. "It was not a press conference—it's a television show. *Our* television show, and the press has no business on the set." Ailes created his own media circus and it worked like a charm. Nixon would win the election and shortly afterward would fire Ailes for insulting him in an interview with reporter, Joe McGinnis in The Selling of the President 1968.

Ailes would not stay away from politics long. After a brief stint in stage productions and documentaries, he would find a way to merge his obsession for theater and politics. He told the Washington Post in 1972; "I know certain techniques such as press releases that look like a newscast, so you use it because you want your man to win."[4]

Translation:
I know how to spit out whatever bullshit I want and make it look like it's legitimate news. I fool people into believing this crap because all I care about is my guy winning.

In 1974, he would find a job where he could put such talent to good use. He landed a job at Television News Incorporated. It was a right wing network with a cool motto. "Fair and Balanced."[4]

Of course this would be the motto of Fox News years later. It was a fair and balanced network alright. Joe Coors was the super conservative genius that created the debacle that came to be known as TVN. He would come with the bright idea to sneak his far-far-far right wing views into all the news broadcasts. He would provide news clips that stations could use without credit, and he would sweeten the pot by making the cost of production dirt cheap. Then when all the affiliates would begin grabbing the discounted clips like Rush Limbaugh stuck in traffic without a bottle of pills to chug, the master plan would come together. As Coors would so eloquently put it, TVN will gradually, subtly, slowly inject our philosophy in the news--cue evil laughter: ha ha...ha ha ha...ha ha ha ha ha!!! Yep, this sounds um, fair and balanced to me.

Some employees referred to the network as a propaganda machine. The ideological pressure from the idiots who ran the network caused a revolt by the professional journalists who thought they could be fair and balanced until they were told otherwise.[4]

Ailes would be called in to save the day and command the newsroom. Under his fair and balanced leadership, TVN would sign an open ended contract to produce propaganda for the federal government. This would include news clips and even scripts to the U.S. Information Agency.[4]

It's a pure coincidence of course, that Mr. Fair and Balanced would do this with a Republican in the White House. Of course Ailes claimed that there was no conflict of interest with the Ford Administration. How reassuring.[4]

Talk about big government, huh? Clips and scripts, but um...fair and balanced. This is a pretty good idea of the type of mindset such a fair and balanced leader must have. It gets better though.

TVN would collapse in 1975. "They were losing money

and they weren't able to control their journalists.", said Kerwin Swint, author of Roger Ailes' biography titled Dark Genius."

It was a huge disappointment for Ailes. His right wing theatre just went up in smoke in the blink of an eye.

Ailes was determined however, to jumpstart another fair and balanced propaganda machine. It would take a while, but he would pull it off and he would learn from his mistakes of the past. There was a formula. Generating money and control of the journalists had to be a must. No more revolts.[4]

After the collapse of his right wing fantasy network, Ailes became immersed in political consulting. The same manipulating tactics that he used to put Nixon in power would also be used on behalf of Ronald Reagan and George H.W. Bush.

Ailes would first oversee the legendary "Morning in America" campaign in 1980 that launched Reagan into the White House. When Reagan's age became an issue "in his bid for re-election" it was Ailes who suggested to Reagan on numerous occasions *forget the facts and figures* and stick with themes.[4]

It was the same for George Bush (Part 1). Bush was seen by many as weak and he had some major baggage he was toting. The Iran Contra scandal was like an albatross around his neck. Ailes would advise Bush to shrug the facts and go on the offensive. That's the mindset of the ring leader of the conservative movement. To hell with logic and data. That's not how you get elected.[4]

You gain power by showing you're a fighter. You appeal to people's frustrations. That's Fox News and their loyal following today. The stupid ass liberal media wants to pounce on facts all the time. Screw facts. Let's get emotional.

That's exactly what Ailes wanted and Bush, willing to do almost anything to get elected, followed suit. Everything from a rigged interview and disgusting altercation with Dan Rather in 1988, to a smear campaign against Governor Michael Dukakis that dripped with racist overtones.

The tactics for the smear campaign did get Bush elected, but it would end up backfiring on Ailes down the road. The first time however, was the charm. Ailes would throw convicted murderer, Willie Horton in the face of Michael Dukakis every chance he got. Horton escaped while on a weekend furlough from prison and would attack a couple by stabbing the man and raping the woman. Dukakis was the governor of Massachusetts at the time. Ailes bragged to reporters, "the only question is whether we depict Willie Horton with a knife in his hand or without it."[4]

Ailes was a smart guy and he knew that this tactic could very well backfire. So, he decided to be a bit more subtle. After experimenting with a few takes and deciding they were a little too racist he settled on one that seemed just right.[4]

The ad would show a Black prisoner wearing an afro

that had the unmistaken resemblance to Horton. The message was clear: If Dukakis becomes president, he's going to be soft on Black murderers while they roam the streets and kill innocent White people.

Bush would win the White House. Ailes meanwhile, would continue to use the Willie Horton tactic against Democrats. It backfired in 1989 while working for Rudy Giuliani. David Dinkins would become the first Black mayor of New York by deciding to make Ailes himself the target. He would give Ailes the well-deserved label of "the master of mud".[4]

Giuliani would get smashed and the "master of mud" went into a real slump. He started losing elections left and right. So Mr. Mud made a grand exit from politics in 1991. He told the New York Times that he had been in politics for 25 years and that it had been a detour. He wanted to get back into entertainment and his "corporate clients".[4]

He was lying. This, of course, was no big deal. This just means Ailes was staying true to form. He knew that his reputation as Mr. Mud could be a drag for the Bush re-election bid so he did what any smart scumbag would have done. He didn't take a formal role with the campaign, but he was the driving force behind the scenes.

He did it all for Bush. Prepared him for speeches, devised his strategy for the campaign, etc. Through it all, Ailes continued to lash out at the liberal media. He felt Bill Clinton had way too many press secretaries. Ooh, that stupid liberal media.[4]

This time, the smear campaign was against Bill Clinton. As Tim Dickinson wrote, "from his office in Manhattan, Ailes advised the campaign to spin Clinton's graduate school train trip to Moscow into a tale of Manchurian candidacy." Let's hear three cheers for the famous Joe McCarthy strategy!!!

Bush carried out the strategy every chance he got. Attacking Clinton everywhere from Larry King Live, to regular stump speeches, to screaming it from the rooftops: "He's a communist sympathizer or maybe even a communist agent, just don't vote for him, aghhh!!!"

Bush tried his best. He said screw the facts, distorted the truth, and attacked Clinton with a petty smear campaign that resembled a fourth grader trying to start rumors against the dodge ball captain for hitting him first. In the end, the Ailes strategy would fail. The Clinton machine rolled over Ailes and Bush. Like he did after most ass whippings, Ailes decided to *act* like he was leaving politics for good. But he didn't.

Ailes would help launch a few T.V. shows and one year after his so called retirement he would sign a secret deal with RJ Reynolds and Phillip Morris. The two tobacco companies wanted him to do everything possible to derail Bill Clinton's central policy objective. Clinton's healthcare bill also known as Hillarycare would be paid for in part by putting a tax on cigarettes. Big tobacco was determined to fight Clinton tooth and nail. To succeed, they hired the dirtiest player in the game.[4]

Internal memos show just how low Ailes was willing to

go. He wanted, at one point, to see if Phillip Morris could create a group called the "Coalition for Fair Funding of Healthcare". This phony so called independent group could produce propaganda ads.

Then he really hits his stride. Ailes and tobacco companies flooded Congress with angry phone calls from...well, Ailes and the tobacco companies. Then, as Tim Dickinson puts it, "To gin up the appearance of a grass roots uprising, busing 17,000 employees to the White House for a mass demonstration."

Ailes also used the right wing media to perfection. He went and got his buddy, Rush Limbaugh to join in on the covert operation. Ailes brought Limbaugh into the world of T.V. and the two had grown quite fond of each other.[4]

One internal memo reads: "RJR has trained 200 people to call in shows, a packet has gone to Limbaugh. We need to brief Ailes." Ailes succeeded. The covert operation worked and the fake uprising against Clinton was nothing more than a combination of big tobacco, right wing media—Ailes and Friends—and obedient Republicans in Congress who followed their lead. It was the prelude to the Tea Party. Good old patriots protesting against the Clinton policies. They wanted their country back...nope.[4]

Look again, it's just corporate America using Roger Ailes and his silly ass foot soldiers to derail a piece of legislation that could have saved the lives of millions of Americans who died because they couldn't afford health insurance. Hey, at least our cigarettes still cost the same! Smoke it up, America! Look out RJ Reynolds!! Making billions of dollars isn't enough. Let's fool America so our guy can win. Such patriots, huh?

During this time period Ailes would get a gig at CNBC. It's only right, you see. Corporate America must take care of their own. Profits soared at CNBC thanks to Ailes. He put together a juggernaut and developed stars on the network. While doing this, big tobacco kept him on the payroll for 5,000 dollars a month. They called on him every time they needed some propaganda to save them from being regulated. They would call Ailes, who would then call Limbaugh, who then rallied the circus...I mean, troops.[4]

Despite having such a great gig at CNBC, Ailes wasn't having fun anymore. He wanted even more power. He wanted the power to shape public opinion. He wanted the station to be a reflection of him...on everything. But it wasn't happening. Ailes came to disagree with developments that were taking place so he secured his release from his contract.[4]

It was this release that allowed Ailes to leave and team up with a man who would give him all the tools he would need to make his right wing dreams come true.

Rupert Murdoch had already tried to buy CNN and failed. He had tried several times on putting together some type of fake news show that he could air through News Corp. affiliates. One of them was supposed to disguise itself as a straight face news program, but was designed to feature weekly attack-and-destroy missions on liberal politicians.[4]

Murdoch, it seemed, wanted a counterweight to the left wing biased of CNN. As managing editor of the first version of Fox News, Dan Cooper put it: "There's your answer right there to whether Fox News is a conventional news network or whether it has an agenda."

Murdoch was crazy about Ailes, and both men had a lot in common. A former deputy of Murdoch said, "Rupert is driven by a two-fold dynamic: power and money. He had a lot of business reasons to shake up Washington, and he found in Roger the perfect guy to do it." Rupert had plans for expansion and didn't need regulation minded liberals in his business. Roger Ailes, on the other hand, just wanted the power to shape a radical agenda and money seems to have come with it. All the more better.[4]

Ailes was a good student of history. He would not repeat the mistakes of the TVN debacle. And whatever Roger wanted to make this thing work, Rupert gave it to him. Murdoch was ready to invest hundreds of millions at the request of Roger. Ailes seemed to love Murdoch's "nerve" and praised the venture as *true capitalism*.[4]

Ethics would not get in the way of the political agenda this time. He brought dozens of loyal staffers in. People who felt like they owed Roger Ailes. Then he gave a "litmus test" to current staffers. Whoever was not conservative enough got the boot. Ailes also brought in a shitload of newcomers so that he could shape and mold the network into his own image. Grooming them to be an extension of himself. To oversee the young puppets, Ailes brought in John Moody. Moody was conservative veteran of Time magazine.[4]

According to Scott Collins in "Crazy Like a Fox", Ailes confessed one of the problems we have to work on here together when we start this network is that most journalists are liberals and we've got to fight that. "Reporters understood that a right wing bias was hard-wired into what they did from the start. All outward appearances were that it was just like any other newsroom, claims a former author. But you knew that the way to get ahead was to show your color—and that your color was red." No, she's not talking about being a blood. She's talking about the color of the Republican Party.

So, you get ahead by being...fair and balanced? Hell no. You got ahead by showing that you were not just conservative but that you were a mini Roger Ailes. Programmed to spew whatever he felt to be tasteful.

Fox would become a force, but nothing first exemplified it's muscle like the 2000 election. According to a study by the University of California, Fox News shifted about 200,000 ballots to Bush in areas where voters had access to the political machine. It gets better though. Ailes and his team at Fox News had an agenda, and that agenda was to do anything possible to push Bush to victory.[4]

Mr. Fair and Balanced would tap a guy by the name of John Prescott Ellis to head the networks "decision desk". On the night of the election, Mr. Ellis was the consultant who would call states for either Bush or Gore. Seems innocent enough so far, right? Actually, no.[4]

It seems Mr. John Prescott Ellis is none other than Bush's first cousin. He was a columnist at the Boston Globe who had rescued himself from covering the campaign. Ellis would tell his readers, "There is no way for you to know if I am telling you the truth about George W. Bush's presidential campaign, because in his case, my loyalty goes to him and not to you."[4]

Tim Dickinson put it best, "In any newsroom worthy of the name, such a conflict of interest would have immediately disqualified Ellis. But for Ailes, loyalty to Bush was an asset." Ailes actually tried to make this stunt seem legitimate at a House hearing after the election. "We at Fox News do not discriminate against people because of their family connections." Ah yes, good old Roger. So fair and balanced. Why would family connections mean anything? Even if it's a family member who removed himself from covering the campaign while he was at the Boston Globe because he admitted his loyalty was to his cousin and not his readers when it came to this election. Its gets even better folks. It's one thing to have a biased cousin covering the election. It's another thing when the biased cousin would trigger one of the most controversial moments in the history of U.S. elections.

Ellis and Bush were in constant contact throughout the night. Then after midnight, numbers began to flow in that showed Bush with an extremely slim lead. Ellis, for some strange reason, decided that this was enough proof to declare Bush the winner.[4] This made about as much sense as declaring the Patriots the winner of the Super Bowl because they had a one point lead over the New York Giants...*at half time*!!!

Florida was still rated too close to call by the vote

tracking consortium used by all the networks. Yet, good old biased John Prescott Ellis declared Bush the winner. To say that this was premature would be a huge understatement.[4] Remember the Patriots had a one point lead at half-time in the Super Bowl? Did I mention that?

Brit Hume would follow orders and announce Bush to be the winner at 2:16 a.m. This move caused every other network to go into panic mode. Everybody thought Fox had beat them to the big story. Actually that wasn't the case at all. Fox "created" the big story.[4]

Every other network quickly followed suit and just like that...Bush wins! That was the headlines in the morning papers. As Dan Rather would point out, "We'll never know whether Bush won the election in Florida or not. But when you reach these kinds of situations, the ability to control the narrative becomes critical."

Yes, the narrative was not just critical, it was the deciding factor. Ellis immediately seized control of the narrative and put everyone in America under the impression that Bush won the election.

Tim Dickinson wrote, "Dwell on this for a moment: a "news" network controlled by the GOP operative who had spent decades shaping just such political narratives — including those that helped elect the candidate's father — declared George W. Bush the victor based on the analysis of a man who had proclaimed himself loyal to Bush over the facts."

As Rep. Henry Warren would later say, "Of everything

that happened on election night this was the most important impact. It immeasurably helped George Bush maintain the idea in people's minds that he was the man who won the election."[4] Talk about fair and balanced, huh?

It gets even better. After doing everything possible to tip the election into Bush's favor, Ailes and Bush kept close contact with each other. According to Tim Dickinson, quoting a source from Fox News, "The senior-level editorial people believe that Roger stayed on the phone everyday with Bush. He gave Bush the same kind of pointers he used to give George H.W. Bush—delivery, effectiveness, and political coaching."

It seems Ailes was even using Karl Rove as a liaison to communicate with Bush at times. After the election, Ailes kept Bush on point and then kept the viewers on his side. Ailes would give Bush the game plan and then advise his fair and balanced stooges...I mean journalists, to explain to the public why Bush's game plan should be supported. Each morning Ailes would give the spin to his trusted goffers like John Moody and Brit Hume.[4]

As Tim Dickinson points out, Moody then posted a memo with explicit instructions on how to slant the day's news coverage according to the agenda of those on "the second floor" as Ailes and his loyal vice presidents are known."[4]

Moody would consistently advise the staff on how to champion the president. While making sure the Bush-Ailes agenda was being carried out. Moody also made sure the fair and balanced journalists highlighted John Kerry's flaws. Whether it was his voting record or the way he combed his hair. Moody instructed the staff very clearly on how to bash Kerry.[4]

Coincidently, the attacks by Fox on Kerry happened to fall right in line with Bush's accusations against the Massachusetts senator. Okay, it's not a coincidence. Scott McClellan was the press secretary for Bush at the time. He would admit, "We, at the White House, were getting them talking points." Well, I'll be…now, I know there must be some type of explanation for a fair and balanced network to be receiving talking points from the president and feeding them to their viewers. Actually there isn't.[4]

Fox News was not just in bed with the Bush White House. They were his voice to the American people, and he was the voice of Roger Ailes on many fronts. If someone wanted to be a voice for the Bush Administration then that's fine. America is a free country. But this is different. Fox deceived it's viewers by *acting* like an unbiased source of information that's supposed to be fair and balanced. But it's not, because it had an agenda to carry Bush and Bush had an agenda to do their (Fox's) bidding. It was perfect. Murdoch was making money off of his network, Ailes was shaping public opinion toward his own agenda and Bush had a 24-7 propaganda machine, free of charge. What a wonderful world.[4]

The network is unfair toward anyone who's not a Republican and damn sure wasn't balanced. When Bush won re-election, Rupert Murdoch and Roger Ailes celebrated inside the control room of Fox News until 3:00 a.m. The older male, scumbag version of Lavern and

Shirley. They had a blast.[4]

Fox has continued to grow stronger as a political machine. Just like the fair and balanced network was committed to building support for the Bush agenda, it has been just as committed to demonizing Barack Obama for everything and anything. As Tim Dickinson wrote, "Fox News went all out to convince it's White viewers that he was a Marxist, a Muslim, a Black nationalist, and a 1960's radical.

Ailes himself has openly joked and poked fun at the president's name while making it no secret at all that he opposes him in every way possible.[4]

The morning talk show, Fox and Friends, gets their talking points straight from Ailes. Steve Doocy and Gretchen Carlson are the two puppets who first claimed that Obama was "raised a Muslim."[4] The key piece of evidence for this claim was um...um...that Roger Ailes got a hold of...well, there is no evidence for this. It must have just seemed fair and balance at the time.

Several former co-workers for Fox have openly admitted that the Obama era has caused Fox to ramp up its propaganda more than ever. Changes inside the network showed Fox pushing even harder to the right so that the channel could be in complete opposition to Obama on everything.[4]

One of the biggest moves was when Roger Ailes hired Glenn Beck from CNN. Beck was a pretty normal guy at CNN. He even seemed to be interesting at times. Then

Beck transformed from normal to rambling idiot. Of course, money will do that to you.[4]

As Tim Dickinson pointed out, Ailes hired Glenn Beck away from CNN to set him loose on the White House. During his contract negotiations Beck recounted that Ailes confided that Fox News was dedicating itself to impeding the Obama administration. "I see this as the Alamo", Ailes declared.[4]

Now a few things to look at right here. The first is that Ailes points this out to Beck during the contract negotiations. Glenn Beck attacked Obama's agenda relentlessly. One has to ask what Beck's true motivations were? Was it really core convictions or was it a fat paycheck? He was not brought to Fox to be fair and balanced. He admits that he was brought there because Ailes wanted to impede the Obama Administration. Beck didn't act like a demented weirdo while he was at CNN but he becomes the attack dog at Fox. Why? Is it because he cared more about money while he was at CNN so he suppressed his true feelings? Or is it because Fox liberated him from the shackles of CNN...with more money?

Either way, money seems to be Beck's main motivation and it's clear that Ailes never mentioned during the negotiations that Beck must be fair and balanced to work at Fox. Everybody with a reasonable amount of common sense has always suspected that Beck might just be full of shit, but this should sort of confirm it. The eyeglass wearing geek with the triple chins who wears tennis shoes that never match his pants wasn't crazy after all. He got the money and bullshitted his viewers all the way to the bank.

If Beck had the morals and principles that he claimed to be such an authority on, then wouldn't he just call it like he sees it and stipulate that to Ailes? Maybe he did see it that way...all of a sudden, after a contract negotiation with Ailes. Yeah right.

The second thing to note is that Mr. Fair and Balanced let Beck know from the get-go that this was "The Alamo". All that shit about fair and balanced might sound good on the commercials, but that's not how you regain power. You regain power by tossing facts to the side. Attack and go on the offensive.

Once Ailes pushed his fair and balanced circus even further to the right to be in direct opposition of the new president, then he took advantage of a major opportunity. Just like his days working for the tobacco companies, Ailes decided there was a chance to gin up another grass roots revolt.

The band of...patriots had been stirred into action by the PR whore from Wall St. after he gave his famous speech on CNBC. There was only one problem though. The people who actually gathered was a very small group of middle aged White people who called themselves the Tea Party. Nobody really paid the small group much attention and nobody really knew just what their beef was considering the new president had been in office for only two or three months.

Fox spotted the movement and turned them into a

nationwide force. The Tea Party was about to have one of its first protest on April 15th, 2009. Fox went all out to endorse the rally as "FNC" Tax Day Tea Parties. Journalists from all over the political spectrum were stunned by such a move. Howard Kurtz who used to work for the Washington Post noted, "I don't think I've ever seen a news network throw its weight behind a protest like we are seeing in the past few weeks."[4]

That's because a legitimate "news" network would just cover a story. Not Fox. This was a gift. Unlike the protestors for Clinton's healthcare bill, Ailes would not have to "hire" a grass roots revolt. He would just have to nurture it. He would have to put glaring spotlights on a few hundred people and blow it up to epic proportions to make it seem like this was a reflection of the mass majority of Americans. It worked too.[4]

In August of 2009 when the Tea Party started protesting town hall meetings against healthcare reform, Fox began to take the lead, dishing out instructions on Fox and Friends. The show practically challenged it's viewers to call it's congressman. Just that quickly, in a span of a few months Fox was no longer just endorsing the Tea Party, they were now stirring them and others into action on their behalf.[4]

Then of course, Fox took the smear campaign against the healthcare bill to whole new levels. It's bad enough the damn thing is hard for many people to understand and it's cluttered with all kinds of stuff. Instead of deciphering it for the public, Fox muddied the waters even more by promoting lies about the bill. This was a real disservice to its viewers who might have wanted to actually know about the bill so that they could make an informed choice.[4]

Instead, they heard about death panels and funding for illegal immigrants. Ailes made sure everybody on the Fox News crew was in lockstep on the issue. He even advised everyone covering the story to refer to the "public option" as "government run health insurance".[2]

Tim Dickinson points out the obvious rather well when he said, "The result of this concerted campaign of disinformation is a viewership that knows almost nothing about what's going on in the world." He's right. Fox News viewers are some of the most uninformed people around, but there is a reason for this. These people are not stupid. Misinformed, yes. Stupid? No. The mass majority just love to hear their favorite talking points recited. It's true. If you watch Fox and Friends in the morning then you have pretty much got the major talking points for the rest of the day.

Buy why do they only care about talking points? Because their favorite team is all that matters. Republicans are right and Democrats—if they're not acting like Republicans—are trying to destroy the traditions of this great country. This destroys them too. These noble patriots feel disregarded and looked down upon. Fox News tends to come to the rescue.

As author, Rick Perlstein put it, "What Nixon did—and what Ailes does today in the age of Obama—is unravel and rewire one of the most powerful of human emotions: shame. He takes the shame of people who feel that they are being looked down on and he mobilizes it for political purposes. Roger Ailes is a direct link between the Nixonian politics of resentment and Sarah Palin's politics of resentment. He's the golden thread."[4] Indeed he is.

The political machine that spews lie to its viewers while shamelessly promoting the ideology of Roger Ailes is not just a megaphone for Republicans to run off at the mouth 24 hours a day. It's a fundraising machine for Republicans as well. A good example of this is John Kasich. He was a household name on Fox for a while. He was the host of a show on Fox called Heartland. He also made over three dozen appearances on the network after announcing his interest in running for governor. He was all over the place on Fox. Free airtime and a way to shamelessly raise money. In fact, the network was his platform for raising funds.[4]

Tim Dickinson also notes, "News Corp. itself chipped in 1.26 million to the Republican Governors Association, making it one of the largest single contributors to the club Kasich was seeking to join."

Rupert Murdoch didn't even try to hide it saying, "it was driven by my friendship with John Kasich."[4]

John Kasich would go on to win the race and become governor of Ohio. He is a Republican, but as Dickinson points out, "Kasich might be understood as the first candidate of the Fox News Party.[4]

Karl Rove has also used the network American Crossroads. This patriotic group is funded by Rove and raises money to create a bunch of smoke screens and lies that help Republicans win elections. These are just a few examples of many.[4] Fair and balanced? Not even close.

As one former media critic put it, "The question is no longer whether Fox News is an arm of the GOP, but whether it's the torso."[4]

Fox made over 800 million dollars in one year. Rupert Murdoch loves the money. So does Roger Ailes who's making about 24 million a year. But Ailes is having fun again. He's back in politics by using Fox as the ultimate weapon. As long as he keeps profits up, Murdoch will let him have his way.[4]

Ailes is a political operative who has discovered the most easy and profitable way to advance his political agenda. He helped transform the Tea Party from a small comical movement into an electoral force. Roger Ailes is really the central component to the movement. He nurtured them into a force. Now they march to it. They protest for it. They believe it and they embrace it. Facts don't matter. He gives them the ammo that's needed to stir them up.[4]

Then he uses Fox as a fundraiser for Republican politicians and a 24-7 platform for themselves to sell books, host shows, or win re-election. In return they do what he says, because if not their ass is grass. The worst thing that can happen for a "Republican" is to be slammed on Fox News. That's political death for a conservative. The Tea Party—Roger's foot soldiers—will run their asses straight out of Washington.[4]

Here's a good example of how all this ties in together.

Wall St. execs lobby their favorite Republicans on deregulating certain areas of the market. These execs fund the campaigns of these clowns so they expect their way. The politicians promote the deregulation through Fox News.

Ailes gets the word and puts his little puppets...I mean journalists and talking heads on notice as to how he wants them to spin it. They spin it and feed it to their viewers. Many of which are members of the Tea Party who take this information and go absolutely hysterical. They go ahead and march for the deregulation that they know absolutely nothing about or who it benefits. They just know Fox gave them some ammo to fight that Marxist president, so it's time to fight.

Another scenario is when those Wall St. execs or "tobacco" companies decide to bypass the middleman and go straight to Roger Ailes himself, who then let's his fellow Republicans in Congress know what the agenda is and while they carry it out and spread the word throughout Capitol Hill...the Fox News stooges...I mean idiots...I mean pundits get the spin and blast it all day.

So, we see how this works hand in hand. It's the perfect marriage. Corporate America and the warped social agenda of disgruntled Reaganites brought together, working in perfect harmony through the man that gives them both what they want by receiving exactly what he wants.

I could go on and talk about the fact that Rupert Murdoch now despises Ailes or the fact that Ailes is a nut who thinks gays and Muslims are out to kill him, but I won't. That's story is for another book.

Just know this for now folks. The so called "liberal media" has not come clean when they call Fox conservative "leaning". That would be one a hell of a "lean". Fox is a bullshit propaganda network that spews one sided horseshit to its viewers.

As former Fox commentator, Jane Hall put it, "He (Roger Ailes) is Fox News." It's his vision. It's a reflection of him." When you're watching Fox News all you're seeing is a bunch of mini Roger Ailes clones. Programmed to serve his own interest. It's about the money and power of a self-serving lowlife who now pulls the strings of the conservative movement. As former speech writer, David Frum put it, "Republicans originally thought that Fox worked for us. Now we're discovering that we work for Fox."[4]

The conservative movement is a reckless, dangerous vehicle going full speed down a road they hope will lead them back to power. It might, but they might cause a huge wreck in the process and the American people will be the ones hurt by it. The engine however, that makes that vehicle run is the mastermind to their media fantasy land. This same idiot helped zoom the car into a ditch once before. The "master of mud" knows about cars but he's a lousy driver when he gets behind the wheel.

8 | THE ORACLE OF ALL ASSHOLES

When Barack Obama campaigns for re-election his main slogan might be, "I am not Mitt Romney." Mitt Romney's main slogan might be, "I am not Mitt Romney." Whoever Mitt Romney might be, *he* might not know. Politicians lie and flip flop all the time but Mitt Romney has clearly brought flip flopping to a whole new level. He's like the Michael Jordan of flip flopping. One of the things that make his flip flops so unique is that he's flipped and flopped on everything he's ever proclaimed. He's done more flipping and flopping than Rush Limbaugh's stomach did after he ate all those delicious Percodan that maid brought him and he obviously mistook for chocolate chip cookies. Which is believable, you know. Rush loves chocolate chip cookies the way he loves...well, drugs.

Anyway, Mitt Romney will have to campaign against two people to win the White House, himself and Obama. This might turn out to be difficult but only time will tell.

His audacity, however, is almost admirable. Imagine telling a room full of people that your favorite sport is football, your favorite food is chicken, and your favorite movie is Gone with the Wind. Then you step out of the room for an hour and come back saying your favorite sport is basketball, your favorite food is fish, and your favorite movie is Rambo.

The room full of people is a bit caught off guard, and they tell you flat out that your list of favorites has changed. You then boldly declare: I never liked football, chicken or Gone with the Wind. In fact, you people must be mistaken because I have never even seen Gone with the Wind. I am allergic to chicken and football is just way too brutal. Then you simply rattle on about your new list as if nothing happened.

It's so outrageous that the people in the room begin to second guess their own sanity. This is pretty much how Mitt Romney is building his own voting bloc. "You people must have mistaken me." His other strategy is really smooth if I do say so myself. It goes something like this: Okay America, I might be an uptight, out of touch liar, but I know how to run an economy way better than the president. I am telling the truth this time. Honestly, I will never flip flop on this and admit that I know absolutely nothing about running the world's largest economy. Nope I lie, but not about this.

Mitt Romney's flip flops are so well documented that I won't bother to bore you with a detailed recap. Instead, we will just quickly gloss over his past ideology.

While Governor of Massachusetts, he made the state the first to limit carbon dioxide emission from power plants because he accepted the scientific proof that humans contribute to climate change. But now he says: "My view is that we don't know what's causing climate change on this planet." He no longer endorses methods to reduce carbon dioxide emissions either.

As governor he refused to pursue politics that would restrict a woman's right to abortion, and didn't have a problem with Roe vs. Wade as law of the land. But now it's a whole new ballgame. Now he has a big problem with Roe vs. Wade and feels it should be reversed. He says it's "bad law and bad medicine". He is now anti-abortion...all the way. He's sure of it...for now, I guess.

While governor, he also helped introduce the country to universal healthcare by using an individual mandate as the centerpiece of the legislation. Now he just hates, hates, hates the idea of an individual mandate. He vows to repeal Obamacare if he becomes president because he just hates the bill because...it looks so much like his? Whatever the case, he now hates the mandate.

It gets better though. Several years ago, he supported an immigration reform package authored by Senators John McCain and Ted Kennedy. The package included a form of amnesty. He went a step further in 2006 when he endorsed the idea of allowing at least some undocumented immigrants to stay in the country "beginning a process of registering for citizenship." But now he's against any type of amnesty for illegal immigrants and vows to veto the Dream Act if it was to make it to his desk should he become president.

The list could go on—gun rights, gay rights, a flat tax—but you get the picture. This guy is just a flip and flop away from changing on anything. When he ran against Ted Kennedy for his U.S. Senate seat in the mid 90's, Mitt campaigned as a liberal Republican to try and oust the liberal lion. That whole liberal thing didn't work out so he campaigned as a moderate when he ran for governor. That worked and he won. So he tried the same formula when he ran for president in 2007. But he lost, so being a moderate got nowhere that time. This time, he knows conservatives want a conservative and he knows why. It's the same reason he's campaigning as a conservative, because that seems like the winning formula. If only he could run from his past. People just keep bringing up the fact that he's changed on everything so much that he could have ran for president as a Democrat. But he's not a Democrat. He's a Republican and a damn conservative one...according to him...now.

These silly ass facts seem to be a hindrance to Mitt's mission. How in the hell is he supposed to fight "Obamacare" if people keep comparing it to "Romneycare". People are always comparing the two and Mitt just seems to hate, hate, hate that. I mean, so what if they are almost the exact same plan? I would tell you that Romney's righteous indignation is understandable but then I would have to flip flop later and admit it's really not.

Rick Santorum constantly tried to point these sort of things out during the GOP debates. Romney was completely unfazed and instead of justification for his past, he would turn right around and hammer Santorum for the fact that he too had not fully repented from his past transgressions against conservative purity.

Yes, Mitt Romney is not only campaigning as a conservative Republican. Nope, he's now a really, really conservative Republican. He's like Ronald Reagan, only without the charm, charisma, and oratory skills. Okay, maybe more like Barry Goldwater. Only Barry was a consistent conservative unlike Romney or Reagan. Okay, he's conservative though.

He's even strong on border control now. Being a "true conservative" that he is, he bashed the conservative governor of Texas, Rick Perry for instituting "magnets" for illegal immigrants. After looking up what the word meant, Governor Perry was deeply hurt.

You see, according to Romney's logic, illegal immigrants don't risk their lives crossing the border to escape mass poverty and lunatic drug cartels. They do it because college is way cheaper in the U.S. than it is in Mexico. Look out Texas A&M! The next starting quarterback in the Alamo Bowl just might be from Tijuana!! That's a clever scheme putting all those magnets in place. Nothing upgrades a college like shrewd recruiting tactics.

He's even conservative on foreign policy now. He's ready to practically start a trade war with China, bomb Iran, and duke it out with our number one adversary...Russia. Every hero needs a "formidable" foil, I suppose. It's not like Russia doesn't act like delusional numbskulls who are still having flashbacks of the Cold War. It's just that it was a bit of a letdown that he picked them to be our "number one adversary" in the world. But hey, whatever floats your boat. I would have thought something like...um, I don't know...Al-Qaeda maybe!!!

You might be thinking that conservatives are disgusted with such a transparent anomaly. Some experts even suspect they won't come out and support him enough to win the election. They will. Conservatives might grumble and complain, but they will turn out in full force. As I have said throughout this book, their goal is power.

It doesn't matter who the GOP candidate is. They have made it clear that their goal is to win.

You would think Romney might have sucked some of their enthusiasm out. Just a little, huh? Not in the least. You see, in a sense Romney is the perfect GOP candidate. He embodies everything there is to dislike about today's conservative movements. He's a flip flopper. Guess what? Conservatives have been doing that for years. Ronald Reagan campaigned as an anti-tax candidate when he ran for president. George Bush (Part 1) was a moderate who campaigned as a conservative who governed like a moderate.

After the hard right winger Newt Gingrich brought the party through a fiasco, they got behind the moderate Bush who created a complete identity crisis when he governed like he had lost his mind. When John McCain lost, being moderate was a non-starter this go round. This type of schizophrenic, split personality puts Romney in his element.

He tried to win as a liberal and lost. Being a little less liberal—moderate—worked once, but not the second time. Now he's "100 percent conservative", as he put it. He truly reflects their values. They will vote for him at all costs. It doesn't matter if they like him. Hell, do you really think they liked Nixon? Then again, *Nixon* might not have liked Nixon.

Mitt Romney's Republican victory in the primaries was a close resemblance to the typical Nixonian campaign strategy. He bludgeoned his opponents with negative ads. He pounded them with relentless attacks and around the clock propaganda to divert attention from his own track record. The message was simple: You might not like me because I am a lying, uptight, out of touch elitist, but I can win. They can't.

He's the kind of candidate that conservatives salivate at the mouth for. He will degrade himself at all costs just to win. Even if it means telling a room full of people in Mississippi, "Mornin' ya'll. I just ate some cheesy grits and biscuits for breakfast." Or walking up to a Black baby as he did in 2008 and said, while grabbing his necklace, "Wow, that's some nice bling-bling."

It would have been so gratifying had that little baby jumped straight up out of the stroller and bitch slapped him in his face for being such a stereotypical piece of shit.

It's not completely his fault though. Mitt Romney is a politician, but he's not a very good one. He has no idea on how to relate to average people. It's not because he's rich. Many rich people are likeable and fun to be around. Romney is not likeable or fun to be around. This is because he has a hard time disguising the fact that he really doesn't give a shit about other people and their suffering.

It's like having a schoolteacher that is awkward or out of touch with his or her students. There's something behind it. It's something more than just being shy or not being a people person. If that were the case you wouldn't be a schoolteacher in the first place. Students pick up on it when a teacher is not dedicated. Those are the symptoms for such lack of dedication. This disconnect is noticeable.

It's the same for Mitt Romney. He's not some shy antisocial guy. He's a politician. He has no problem with shaking hands and kissing babies. For him the problem comes with connecting. It's not because his jokes suck— which they do. It's his complete stupidity concerning the middle class. It comes out when he speaks to them about them. His lack of empathy for the people he hopes to govern allows him to change his ideology whenever it's convenient. It doesn't' matter that these issues affect people. He is disconnected from such worries.

Nothing reflects this more than his economic ideology. Amazingly, many voters feel he would do a good job of running the economy. His economic ideology, however, truly sheds light on who he is and what he stands for. It also sheds light on how out of touch he really is with middle class America. He suddenly supports supply side economics. He suddenly sees the light in cutting taxes that don't pay for themselves. He's suddenly embracing an economic ideology that would make Herbert Hoover salute while embracing a budget that would make Barry Goldwater blush. His economic ideology is the typical conservative economic ideology. So, through his economic agenda we now can get a glimpse of his social agenda.

His "gaffes" might cause us to *suspect* that he doesn't care about the poor and the middle class. His own economic blueprint <u>confirms</u> it.

Romney plans to spark the economy by enacting an "across-the-board" twenty percent rate cut for every person. He wants to "repeal the alternative minimum tax", and he wants to abolish the death tax. Here's where it gets really good. He said that he would lower the corporate tax rate to 25 percent, make the R&D tax credit permanent, and end the repatriation tax.

The "across-the-board" tax cut might sound really fair at first, but it's not. In fact, it's really not across-the-board", it's trickle-down economics all over again. More tax cuts for the rich and mere crumbs for the rest of the country. A tax policy center study showed the exact impact of this so called flat tax or "across-the-board" tax cut.

The poorest 20 percent of Americans would get (drum roll please) 78 dollars more!!! Wow!! Talk about being able to afford that operation you've been putting off. Stockpile that for five years and bingo...you got tickets to the Saints game.

Those right there in the middle would get an extra 791 dollars a year. That's like an extra $16.37 a week if you give or take a few pennies. I can appreciate an extra $16.00 a week. It won't encourage me to spend a whole lot more, but it's something.

Meanwhile, the wealthiest 0.1 percent would receive a whopping 264,000 more. So, while the poor get enough to afford an extra candy bar and the middle class get enough to say that they got something, the rich get enough to afford an extra house every year or enough to go and buy several more cars.

To say that this is an "across-the-board" tax cut would be like saying everybody at Burger King received a pay raise because three people were given an extra $15.00 a week, and everybody else was given an extra penny a month. What sense did that even make?

So, the rich get a whopping 264,000 extra. According to a new Tax Policy Center report those tax breaks would add more than 3 trillion dollars to the deficit over the next decade.

Now, we're already debating how to *reduce* the deficit by 4 trillion dollars and here comes Mitt Romney wanting to add 3 trillion to the deficit over the next decade. So, even if we reach the 4 trillion mark, it will just be a smoke screen. We're taking away 4 trillion dollars to finance 3 trillion in tax breaks for the rich. Haven't we seen this before?

Romney's plan to finance huge tax breaks for the rich is

none other than Paul Ryan's plan. Romney has embraced and endorsed the Ryan plan so much that, as of this writing, many speculate that Ryan will be his vice presidential running mate in the upcoming election.

Romney has said on several occasions that he has already adopted Ryan's budget. Ryan's plan showers the rich with tax breaks, while financing those tax breaks by cutting chunks out of the middle class and the poor.

This pretty much means these "across-the-board" tax cuts are just a farce. If the Romney/Ryan plan is implemented it would have devastating consequences on the poor and middle class. The extra $78.00 a year for the 20 percent poorest Americans. You can wipe your ass with it already because it's so small. But after certain programs are chopped into that help these particular Americans, those extra 78 dollars become a huge loss in the Romney/Ryan budget. The same goes for the middle class.

A closer look at Ryan's budget tells us why. Those extra $16.00 a week become obsolete after the Ryan/Romney budget cut into student loans, head start, medical and scientific research, not to mention programs that feed poor people. The damn thing even cuts into weather service. Then of course, Medicaid and Medicare are chopped into. Medicaid is turned into a block program and Medicare is turned into a voucher program. All of this just to finance tax breaks for the rich. I am not even going to bother mentioning the severe cuts to energy, the environment, etc.

So, you have 3 trillion dollars in tax breaks paid for by the middle class and the poor. Paid for by the elderly, the college student, and the guy who's out of work because a CEO on Wall St. knew that if he fumbled the ball our government would bail him out.

Robert Greenstein, President of the Progressive Center on Budget and Policy Priorities, described the impact of the Romney/Ryan budget like this, "It would likely produce the largest re-distribution of income from the bottom to the top in modern U.S. history and likely increase poverty and inequality more than any other budget in recent times (and possibly in the nation's history). He goes on to say specifically, the Ryan budget would impose extraordinary cuts in programs that serve as a lifeline for our nation's poorest and most vulnerable citizens, and over time would cause tens of millions of Americans to lose their health insurance or become under insured."

It should be noted that this guy Robert Greenstein is not big on deficits. In fact, he's a deficit hawk who thinks before he speaks. This is not the observation of some partisan who's trying to just merely discredit Paul Ryan.

The irony of the whole situation is that the massive cuts in the plan don't even rally reduce the deficit. They are just covering the losses made up for the rich.

As journalist, Ed Dionne, Jr. put it, "Rep. Paul Ryan made it absolutely clear that he is not now and never was interested in deficit reduction."

After a couple of years of being lauded by deficit hawks as the man prepared to make hard choices, he proposed a budget that would not end deficits until 2040, but would cut taxes by 4.6 trillion dollars over a decade while also extending all of the Bush tax cuts, adding another 5.4 trillion to the deficit. Ryan would also increase military expenditures, and then eviscerate the rest of the federal government.

Oh yes, Ryan claims he'd make up for the losses from his tax cuts with "tax reform", but offered not a single detail. A "plan" with a hole this big is not a plan at all. Ryan's main interest is in cutting the top income tax rate to 25 percent from the current 35 percent.

His message: Solving the deficit problem isn't nearly as important as (1) continuing and expanding benefits for the wealthy, and (2) disabling the federal government.

Of course Ryan would argue that he has a plan...we just don't know what it looks like and apparently, he doesn't either. Ryan himself said, "As far as tax rates are concerned, that is up to the ways and means to decide which tax expenditures stay, which go, and what are the bond points within the income stream.

Translation:
I am not about to offer any specifics on closing loopholes because I am passing the buck to the ways and means committees. I pulled a number out of thin air, now let them decide how to fix the unrealistic bullshit I just turned into a budget.

Ya see, the huge cuts to domestic programs won't actually lower the deficit because the Romney/Ryan plan has to use those cuts to pay for huge tax breaks for the rich. But Ryan says that's not the case. To pay for the tax cuts he claims he will close 4.6 trillion dollars in loopholes that clutter the tax code. The only problem with this plan is he refused to offer any details or suggest what loopholes should be closed.

Why? Because he has no plans whatsoever of closing any loopholes. Especially 4.6 trillion.

As journalist, Ruth Marcus points out, "On paper, in theory, that number is achievable. The Congressional Budget Office examining the major tax expenditures—such as deductions for charitable contributions or home mortgage interest—found that they added up to some 12 trillion dollars over ten years.

There are other, smaller tax expenditures studded through the IRS code. Yet, each of these expenditures has it's ardent defenders—and an accompanying arsenal of lobbyist. So in the real world, it would be all but impossible to come up with anything near the 4.6 trillion that Ryan would need to avoid losing revenue."

Ruth goes on to say, "If Ryan and his colleagues have a workable proposal to cut tax rates that dramatically without losing badly needed revenue, let's see it. If not, they should stop dangling glittery, expensive promises without showing how they plan to deliver."

The reason Ruth, along with many economist, lobbyist, politicians, etc., find this plan so unrealistic is the reason Paul Ryan was realistic enough not to offer any details of such a plan.

All these so called loopholes are politically toxic for Ryan to touch. This would be like Ryan admitting the Bush tax cuts should expire. This is not just his wealthy ass base of support. This is where the influence of lobbyist is written all over our political courage to raise taxes on billionaires. Do you think he's going to touch things like, the tax free treatment of employer sponsored health insurance? This little loophole amounts to 2 trillion dollars over ten years. He's not going to touch it. Just like he won't touch the deduction for mortgage interest (1.6 trillion). Oh, I get it, he's going to touch up the loopholes that cost about 1 trillion for dividends and capital gains. Yeah right.

These types of loopholes are where the money's at, but believing Republicans will find the courage to close these loopholes is like saying Senator Bernie Sanders of Vermont (self-proclaimed socialist) is going to jump up and demand we cut social security immediately. It's just not going to happen.

It's kind of funny that America's new accountant—Paul Ryan—Mr. Bold Budget Leader would decline to offer a plan. This is the same guy who criticized the president for not offering a plan, but now he himself throws out some numbers and tells us that someone else will make them work. As Ruth Marcus said, "Ryan's plan fails the basic test of responsibility."

The plan is an absolute insult to anyone who has an I.Q. higher than 2. The fact is the savage cuts in domestic spending will only finance tax cuts for the rich. That's it.

Unless Congress pulls off one of the most courageous moves in political history and decides to piss of a shitload of lobbyist and (gasp) rich people. This is doubtful though.

Now, let's give the Romney/Ryan plan the benefit of the doubt. Let's say they somehow close the loopholes—which they're not. You still have a rather warped plan that features massive cuts to the poor and middle class to cover the deficit. You would still have a plan that cuts about 5 trillion dollars in spending to reduce the deficit by about 4 trillion, and I am being modest with that assessment.

In reality, that plan shrinks the size of government and does nothing to the deficit. The bad part is the size of government that shrinks is the part that helps the poor and middle class. The rich meanwhile, will keep the part of government that caters to their wants and needs. It's a budget driven solely off of ideology and campaign contributions. It should go down as the most cowardly, callous, warped, and backwards budget proposal in U.S. history. It makes the one Bill Clinton rejected in the 90's from Newt Gingrich look liberal. Ronald Reagan himself would be like, "Jeeze, these people are either full of shit or they're extremist."

Haven't we tried this before? Weren't we all just really mad with George W. Bush for doing the same thing? Are our memories that short? This is the same method that blew holes in the deficit and failed to stimulate economic growth.

Romney is not stupid, and he knows that this method doesn't work. That's why he rejected this same method in the 90's. So why do it now? Why is he putting such a strain on the poor and middle class just to give the rich an extra 264,000 dollars a year? The answer: He simply doesn't give a shit about the middle class and the poor. His main concern is victory. The people working to get him elected and the super PAC funding his campaign are rich. It's his base and he knows they can launch him into the White House. He's not a humanitarian. He's a businessman and he knows how to win. He made his fortune at Bain Capital.

Romney didn't create jobs. He destroyed them. He was as Rick Perry called him: "A vulture capitalist." Some of the companies he invested in succeeded. Some of them failed. None of them were spared. It was not about the people who Romney fired. It was about keeping his balance sheets straight. He showed no mercy when executing employees. It's not that he hated the people that he fired and it's not like he hated firing people. He just didn't give a fuck one way or the other. His goal was to make money. He didn't create jobs. He made money. He was a businessman and he was good at what he did.

I commend him for making money. He did what he had to do. He should not be scandalized for living the American dream in a law abiding way. Sometimes, you have to fire people. My point is he has a history of serving his own interest and not the interest of others. His personality suggests that he's out of touch with middle America. His economic ideology suggests that he can give a rat's ass about middle America.

To Romney it's a business. Nothing more, nothing less. His own mouth reflects just where his priorities are. Right after winning the Florida primaries he said, "I am not worried about the poor, they have a safety net. I am worried about the middle class. That's about 90 to 95 percent who are struggling."

This is a disturbing statement for a few reasons. First, that same safety net that he's bragging about is the same one he plans to hack into with a double edged ax. Secondly, he must not realize that many in the middle class look pretty poor. Many others are just a paycheck away from being poor. Will he stop worrying about these folks as well once they fall into full-fledged poverty? After all, once that happens the safety net will catch them right? So, no point in worrying about them I guess.

The data says 50 million people are living in poverty. According to Romney's logic, those 50 million are okay. He's worried about those other 90 to 95 percent who are struggling. Is he suggesting that others are struggling more than those 50 million? Isn't this whole statement just a bit absurd?

Think about this for a moment. He proposes the Ryan plan that pretty much mutilates the safety net. Then he says he's not worried about the poor because of that same safety net. Shouldn't the poor become a top priority if you're about to cut off their lifelines?

He's worried about the middle class, but he's not worried about the poor. This makes about as much sense as saying, "I hate my kids, but I love my *entire* family." It's a complicated contradiction. Newsflash folks: The so called middle class is becoming poor! Hello!!!

He campaigns boldly on the fact that if he becomes president he will cut funding for Planned Parenthood. Yet, his own family once donated money to the organization. He's courageous though. He will cut off assistance to an organization that helps over 5 million low-income women. He's not worried about those 5 million women who are poor. They have...um...Planned Parenthood. For now.

Ah yes, so easy to fall in line with such an ideology, because it really fits his make up quite well. It's an ideology that lacks empathy, just like the man who has come to embrace it. He was counting dollars when he was destroying jobs at Bain Capital. Now he's counting votes while destroying programs for the poor and middle class. So what though? He's not trying to save the world. He's trying to win an election, and have a mandate in place to do so.

It's a mandate that would reshape the social and economic landscape. A wealth gap? Try a gulf when he's finished with it. Working class folks...Morning ya'll. Cheesy grits anyone? If it wasn't so calculating and wasn't being done on such a grand scale it would be considered a symptom of lunacy.

Yet, he proposes bold changes. He proposes a courageous budget. An extra 78 dollars a year for the poorest 20 percent of Americans, and an extra $16.37 for those in the middle. It should be considered a scam. These pennies in exchange for murdering programs that help them survive.

This is like saying I am going to buy you a Happy Meal

and buy this rich guy a 264,000 dollar house. To finance this spending I am going to need your car, furniture, some of your wardrobe and some of your food. Now don't complain. I did buy you a Happy Meal, remember? This is precisely why we have a wealth gap the size of the Pacific Ocean. It is <u>not</u> a product of capitalism, it's a product of idiots like Romney.

Of course, Romney is a true capitalist. After all he worked in the private sector, remember? He believes that government should stay out of the way. Let free enterprise take its course. That's why he opposed the auto bailout. It doesn't matter if the bailout saved over a million jobs. It doesn't matter if the auto bailout was a huge success. According to Romney, the government has no business meddling in the private sector. He would know because he worked in the private sector. He's now an expert on the private sector. If this logic is legitimate then Donald Trump is supposed to be his running mate.

That's why Romney also opposed the bank bailout…oh no, he was for the bank bailouts. He said this countless times.

Oh I get it, it's okay to bail out Wall St. but it's not okay to bailout Detroit. The bailout on Wall St. created a sense of dependency for the rich, but it's not okay to bailout the middle class workers who depend on the auto industry to make a living. This isn't a gaffe either. He's said this in several GOP debates and countless speeches. This is not just a double standard, it's absolutely senseless.

Screw the middle class, but bail out the rich. It's

socialism to bailout Detroit but it's okay to bailout the same crooks responsible for the worst economic meltdown in eight decades. Yep, that Mitt Romney. If I didn't know any better I would say that he's biased toward the rich. I mean after all, his own mouth and ideology seem to be a testament to this. Okay I do know, and so do a lot of other people. He is biased toward the rich.

This is Mitt Romney. An ever changing, flip flopping, rich snob who cares about nothing except winning. He has no quarrels about hurting middle America, because he himself won't feel the pain. Actually he will be feeling the benefit after he rewards himself with an extra 264,000 dollar a year tax break. His core convictions is a dollar, and winning. If lining poor people up on the sidewalk and pelting them with eggs gave him a chance to win the election, then he would be out there faster than the word say go slinging dozens of eggs with the velocity and accuracy of Roger Clemens.

He's a wishy-washy, spineless, desensitized coward. He betrayed himself and he's setting the stage to betray the electorate. He's Mitt Romney. Whoever that is. He probably doesn't know. And he probably doesn't care. All he knows is that whoever he is, he's rich. He's rich and he's on the verge of possibly being president. Who really cares about anything else? He certainly doesn't.

If Romney and Paul "Penis Face" Ryan had any inkling of common sense they would give those huge tax breaks to the poor and middle class. If they insist on cutting taxes at a time when the government is digging between couch cushions looking for extra revenue then cut taxes that will actually stimulate the economy.

Those tax breaks would not only end up being a little bit cheaper, they would be paid for by the hatchet job the Romney/Ryan plan propose. It wouldn't be a redistribution of wealth. It would be money going back to those who had it taken out of their pockets with the massive cuts in the first place.

It still wouldn't ease the pain of the cuts, but it would make much more economic sense and it would be a little more fair.

The plan would still suck, but at least it would have some type of logic to it. That's precisely why you won't see these jerkoffs come up with it. This is no longer about sensible. It's about returning to power and imposing a senseless ideology upon the rest of the country. While Wall St. keeps these fools in their back pockets, Fox News will try to sell this garbage to their foot soldiers—the Tea Party—who take it upon themselves to influence the rest of the country with this horseshit.

This is why nobody personifies today's conservative movement more than Mitt Romney. He is the perfect GOP candidate. As they regained their identity after the Bush fiasco, Mitt seems to have regained his identity. He is a rich, lying, selfish, elitist. Looking at him is looking at the movement that will try to push him to victory. Relentless, cold hearted, narrow-minded, quixotic and downright full of shit.

If he wins one could speculate that he might flip flop

again and turn moderate. I doubt it. Even when Republicans try to govern like a bunch of moderates, when they win the White House they still keep their idiotic economic ideology in place. Only one tried to be sensible and truly buck it since 1980. Coincidentally, he's the only Republican to lose re-election in that time span. Of course, that's not the true reason or the sole reason Bush (Part 1) lost re-election, but to conservatives it is.

As far as conservative are concerned, and Mitt Romney as well, he's being elected with a mandate to carry out. We see what that mandate is. It's to push through the Paul Ryan plan. A budget that looks like it was drawn up by George W. Bush and Gordon Gekko.

Whether he's lying now or was lying before is a question he might not know. It's a turn off, but it also makes him dangerous. We really don't know what he's capable of, but we know that he has a specific mandate and it's one that truly hurts the middle class and the poor.

Oh, we know he doesn't like President Obama either. All Obama wants to do is "invest" in the middle class while hiking taxes on the rich. Although just hiking taxes on the rich may not seem like serious deficit reduction, it is appreciated. If he's playing politics then it's nice someone sees the middle class as worth catering to.

I would rather hear someone preach the gospel of the Buffett Rule instead of some heartless, snobbish, economically illiterate, jackass give me a fabricated, backward, illogical lecture on why the rich are job creators and everyone else must sacrifice to pay for their entitlement.

So yes, it's nice to hear somebody point out the big pink fat ass elephant in the room. That the rich have been getting a free ride on the broken backs of the middle class and the poor. If that's playing politics my only complaint is that the president needs to do it even more.

Romney of course, is not playing politics. Good for him. He's just playing games. He's playing games with millions of unemployed Americans. He's playing games with millions of senior citizens and future baby boomers. These are high stakes games. People's lives and futures are at stake. While he does this some wishy-washy, lying pundits like Kathleen "Pelican Face" Parker sugarcoat the facts to seem unbiased. Cowards like this do an absolute injustice to the readers who are trying to make an informed decision about the future of this country.

Meanwhile, Mitt "The Flip" Romney continues to play games. Mitt Romney, whoever he is, has let his priorities show. This is why he's not just the perfect GOP candidate. It's why he deserves a catchy nickname. Something with a ring to it. He might even be able to use it as a campaign slogan.

I've got it. Let's call him Flip Flop. It's perfect. It really brings out his...um...most distinguished attribute.

When you see him just say, "Hi Flip!" or "Good morning, Mr. Flop!" His campaign slogan could even be: Don't let America flop! Vote for Flip! Hmm...he should pay me for this. I think he could really appreciate the humor in such an affectionate pet name.

After all, he does have a great sense of humor. Even his wife says so. They say he was even a prankster in high school. In fact, it was just revealed recently that him and the rest of his buddies held down a student that they had been harassing, beat him up, and cut his hair off. The victim says it was because he was gay.

Mitt—I mean Flip—doesn't dispute the incident. He just doesn't remember. Of course that's believable. "Flip" must have been such a prankster in school that incidents like that happen a dime out of a dozen. The point is at least we know what a scumbag...I mean glorious sense of humor he has.

So, here's to "Flip". He's the perfect guy to represent a perfectly ridiculous, greedy, selfish, lying, moronic, warped, deranged, bullshit movement. Such skills and qualities qualify him to be the oracle of all assholes. I know he's flattered, and honored to have such a deserving title. Congratulations "Flip", you asshole.

9 | CLOSING

Laura Ingram has a face any pet owner would adore. She's really not a bad looking woman at first glance. But, for some reason, her jawline is becoming thicker. It's not your average manly "I am a boxer" jawline. It's the "I can chew through concrete jawline." Ann Coulter's jawline is not half as bad. Ann just has a bullet face, but Laura seems to be morphing into something peculiar. I watched her on Fox News droning on about class warfare and I couldn't help thinking, "If she bites her colleague on the show with those jaws she could lockdown like a pit bull and kill him."

Her jaw was a bit distracting so I tried to pay attention to the venom she was spewing from her snout.

I also couldn't help but wonder how many people bought into her distorted logic. She claimed the same old tired argument. That the president was pitting Americans against each other with class warfare, that liberals want to punish the rich and blah, blah.

I can sort of understand that she's an entertainer. She's making money. That's a good thing, but normal open-minded people might start to trust her stance. Her perspective holds weight. Her audience respects and follows her lead, but for her it's about sensationalizing a perspective to the point of distorting it. Then again most of her audience is probably too unreachable for a new teacher. They might be too invested into their own world view to want to reason with facts that contradict their own logic. It's those few open-minded reasonable people who just want to make an informed decision that sometimes fall victim to idiots like Laura Ingram.

The conservative movement has distorted the narrative so much that many reasonable open minded independents and moderates of both parties are not so sure who to believe and who to trust. The picture becomes fuzzy. They start to wonder, maybe the president is a Muslim, and maybe it matters one way or the other. Maybe we have to turn Medicare into a voucher program or maybe the rich are getting a raw deal…these things can start to go through a person's mind and affect the decision making process.

One of the worst things that can happen is if we start letting misinformed people inform us. What's worse than that, however, is when the informed purposely misinform us. Outlets like Fox News and CNBC are just liars trying to push an agenda. That's it. It's a 24-7 propaganda campaign to protect their own interest.

They love their investments in oil companies and Wall St. megabanks, so they sell us whatever lies are needed to prop up such institutions. Their right wing politicians are bought off by the very same entities. They work together in spewing lies to their warped and demented base who get all stirred up by this propaganda because it lines up perfectly with their already warped social world view.

These people then march and protest with such passion and boldness that the rest of the electorate begin to wonder if they have a point. The whole time Wall St., the media outlets bought by them, and the politicians who benefit across the board sit back and laugh.

A bunch of mindless foot soldiers who crave nothing but having their country back. While these Reaganites/Tea Partiers spur into action to boldly defy the so called elitist, they have no idea that what they are actually doing is the bidding of the very elitist(s) they claim to despise. For these peasants with pitchforks it's all about a *senseless* power grab, justified under the banner of patriotism. For those who sent these fools on a mission it's about a *clever* power grab.

These people line the streets in a stirred frenzy shouting against a deregulation that they will only see the adverse consequences of, not a single benefit. The politician who captivates them into such lunacy has just used such predacious methods for his own glory and his own pockets while his bosses on Wall St. salute his cunning tactics. Then Fox News gets their huge breakoff for replaying the whole incident for several hours and then bringing a dozen talking heads on the air to spin the politician into a modern day hero.

To point these facts out are to be labeled a yenta or worrisome liberal who's clearly out of touch with the traditions of America.

Here's the creepy part though. If the Tea Party did come to realize that they are in fact just foot soldiers for the elitist who are pulling the real power grab, it wouldn't matter. Because there is a mutual interest. Power. That's why this marriage works out so perfectly. These people want their country back and if the rich, good old "Flip", or Fox News can help them then so be it. It's all about power.

What about the rest of us though? Do we just sit on the sideline and *hope* for a normal day? Do we really want to stomach another Bush era? In the end we actually hold the cards but it's up to us to play them. If this next power grab by the conservative movement is successful, it will set a bad precedent.

First, the message to Democrats is going to be obstruct at all cost. Obstruct because it works. Do whatever you gotta do. Sink the economy, vote against the debt ceiling, don't compromise on deficit reduction, oppose no matter what, and create utter chaos while blaming Republicans for everything. Then it might actually work, so we vote them back into power and Republicans go back to using the tactic. While these two sides duke it out the rest of us are collateral damage in a high stakes game of chicken.

The second reason it sets a bad precedent is that we're spoiling conservatives. If they win every time they throw tantrums then chances are they're going to do it again the next time they're not in power. History shows us their pattern. They go into Freakoutville when they are not in charge and each time they become a bit more radical than the last. If they win this time, it would be like endorsing their childish, dangerous tactics. This is the wrong message to send.

We voted Obama into office on the slogan of "Hope and Change", but we underestimated the fight for such change. One man cannot change anything. It's up to us. This upcoming election will decide if radical right wing succeeded or if we want this childish little game to end. This movement of brats and idiots does not want change. They want their country back.

They thrive off of tradition. Did they distort the narrative enough to take it back or is this still our country too? This year will either make or break their spirit (for the moment at least). It will be a victory for Wall St. or it will be a victory for Main St. Will it be a victory for Roger Ailes or will it be a victory for those who need Medicare? Do we take one sluggish step forward or ten steps backwards?

It's not about competing ideologies or talking points. Real lives are at stake. It's not about red or blue. It's about right or wrong. Logic vs. complete lunacy.

It's one thing to have a president whose real methodical and treads cautiously. It's annoying at times, but I can live with it. It's another thing for him to boldly and decisively move in the wrong direction. That can be catastrophic. Remember Iraq? I wish *somebody* would have thought that through a little better.

One message that needs to be made loud and clear to the Tea Party is that it's not just your country anymore!!! The gig is up. This generation will not surrender it back to you. It belongs to Black people, Gay people, Latinos, women and men from all walks of life. So take your rebel flags and hang them all over the place. For you, they are a reminder of a country that *was* just for you. For us, they are a reminder of your defeat. *Our* country, scoot over and let me share it with you. You long for the past, but we have a vision for the future. America is no longer represented by just one group of people. I think I just heard Ann Coulter jump out of a 10th story window in disgust.

This year will be a tone setter. A sounding bell to an opening round. It will decide who gets the edge. A big edge at that.

Stopping them from regaining power will not solve all the country's problems or bring "Morning in America" so to speak. But it could restore a measure of sanity. Which in turn, could lead to progress. It would also send a message to this group that they either adapt to such things like compromise and unity or they can sit on the outside looking in. Stopping them would also derail their economic agenda. It's an agenda that would be a huge setback to the poor and middle class.

"Flip" Romney has made it quite clear what he plans to do. If elected he would be given a mandate to carry it out. We have progressed and come a long way America. It's why we can honestly say that we are the indispensable nation. Now is not the time to get lethargic. We have too much at stake. Our wealth has never had to dictate our morals and principles. Our wealth is a product of those values. Our best days are still in front of us. We just have to be willing to stand up and push forward. It can be exhausting, but it's worth it.

With that said, I must make a confession. I am still visibly shaken by the telecast that I saw earlier. It wasn't just that Laura Ingram is a lying demagogue. It's that she has the strongest jawline that I've ever seen on a woman. Maybe she's on steroids. That might be worth investigating.

If Obama can be a Muslim from another country, then why can't we start an open, sensible dialogue about Laura Ingram's possible steroid use?

She is what the Tea Party is all about. A nonsensical, rambling attack that is laced with stupidity. They have thrown a fit the last three years because they want their country back. For them, it's *their* country. For Wall St., it's *their* unregulated casino. For the Republican politicians, it's a little bit of both. For Roger Ailes, it's *his* agenda. For the rest of us, it's a nightmare.

If an irrational group refuses compromise then it's up to the rest of us to make our voices heard. It's the only way to combat a warped economic ideology that reflects a warped world view. The first step is understanding this. The second step is to act.

It's beneficial to realize that there is something far more creepy to Laura Ingram than her jawline. It's her ability to lie with a straight face. It's her appetite for money and power that unites her to her own kind.

The bond within this movement is tight and they move together on the same page about everything. This is because they don't share a core conviction per se. They speak from a cue. Once they get their cue, they drill it home as the next big talking point.

To care about the country is to care about the people in it. They care nothing about the other people in this country. They simply care about themselves and their own personal agenda. That agenda is to take back the *power*, to be the focal point again. So they will do the bidding of anybody from anywhere to get what they want. They care nothing about the talking points that they proclaim to be so passionate about. They are a bunch of greedy, selfish, warped, perverted, moronic, illogical bigots.

It's the Tea Party. I would like to see Laura Ingram's jaws chew on that!!!

10 | AUTHOR'S NOTE

Here we are in 2014 and many Americans are still disgusted with the partisanship and idiocy taking place in Washington. It might seem like we've won the war but lost the battle. The fact is Obama winning the presidency and voters coming out in droves did help in a few key areas. First, it slowed down the obstructionism and ridiculousness of the extremism within the Republican Party. Secondly, it was a matter of playing defense. It might seem like nothing has gotten accomplished in the last few years. Big things like climate change, gun control and immigration reform have all stalled in Congress. But sometimes it's not what you accomplish, it's what you manage to protect. Medicare is still intact, while other healthcare initiatives are moving forward. Tax rates for the middle class stayed the same, while tax rates for some of the rich finally went back up to something near normal levels. This may not seem like a momentous occasion to celebrate but the fact is our voices did make a difference. It wasn't the win corporate America wanted, instead it was the win Main St. needed.

But what's next? It can't stop right here. It has to go forward. One election does not completely break the back of an extremist movement but it did stop it in its tracks momentarily. One sluggish step forward is always better than ten steps backwards. At one time, the extremism inside of the Republican Party was nothing but a fringe group. In the 1950's and 60's, it was hard to tell the difference between Democrats and Republicans. Most policy issues were pretty much agreed on between both parties with minor differences, but now the fringe elements within the Republican Party are at full force. And whenever there is conflict in our politics, it always effects the economics of the situation.

The best thing to do is not lose heart. With the congressional elections coming up many voters are deflated. One has to get up and dust themselves off and continue to make our voices heard, because if not the little progress that was made in 2012 when Obama won re-election will mean nothing. Wall St. took a minor setback but it doesn't mean they won't try to make a major comeback.

2014 seems like an insignificant year with insignificant issues taking place. Things like Lil Wayne's sexuality and Floyd Mayweather's overhand right against T.I. seems more important than immigration reform right now to many people. The fact is making a paycheck, finding a job, or not losing out on health insurance are more important issues than deciding who to vote for. But it's your vote in

2014 that will definitely lay the foundation for what happens to the middle class in the future. The mass majority of Americans came together and rejected right wing extremism. Just as I predicted, Mitt Romney did embrace the Paul Ryan budget and then the face of the conservative movement (Mitt Romney) flipped and flopped so much that in the middle of one election he went from a severe conservative to an absolute moderate to almost liberal to back to conservative in the span of about a month and a half. It's what the conservative movement does. To keep them moderate and sane the only thing voters can do is go to the ballot box.

2014 should not be considered the destination. Some magical policy initiative should not be considered the answer to all ills. But to leave our kids with the country that we hope for, we should continue to pick up where we left off in 2012. Inequality will only continue to rise and the politics of the moment will only grow more heated again if these things are not done. So there you have it folks. I hope you enjoyed this book and hope you will be on the lookout for the next one especially since my wife will kill me if we don't make any money after all the hours I spent annoying her with the content and if that doesn't inspire you to check out these facts then maybe your own suffering will inspire you. If either of those things still doesn't inspire you, then look no further for inspiration than to Rush Limbaugh. He finally understands the difference between Percodans and chocolate chips. Now if we could just get him to lay off both of them. This is what change looks like!!

ACKNOWLEDGMENTS

"Gryftopia: A Story of Bankers, Politicians, and the Most Audacious Power Grab in American History" was a great source of and provided a wealth of information. It is a recommended must read for anyone trying to gain insight and understanding dealing with the financial crisis of 2008. In many places where Gryftopia was given credit, at times the book was directly quoted and at other times not readily mentioned, it was paraphrased. "The Complete Book of U.S. Presidents, Seventh Edition" was an extremely useful tool and provided excellent guidance in leading me to several other dozen sources of information. A great read for someone who is not trying to get bogged down by a lot of details but instead trying to gain a general knowledge of U.S. history.

"Rising Common Ground, Overcoming America's Color Lines" was another great source of information and was extremely insightful when dealing with the era of reconstruction. Tim Dickinson's "How Roger Ailes Built The Fox News Fear Factory" article featured in Rolling Stone Magazine was the main source of information when referring to Fox News throughout chapter seven, sometimes quoted directly as well as referenced from his article. Though I did a lot of other outside research regarding Fox News, Tim Dickinson's article was found to be the most in-depth. A must read article for those who would like to quickly get to the heart of the details regarding who Fox News really is.

BIBLIOGRAPHY

Matt Taibbi. *Griftopia: A Story of Bankers, Politicians, and the Most Audacious Power Grab in American History*; Spiegel & Grau; 8.7.2011 edition: September 2011[1]

William A. Degregorio, Sandra Lee Stuart. *The Complete Book of U.S. Presidents*, Seventh Edition; Barricade Books, Incorporated: August 2009[2]

Tim Dickinson. *How Roger Ailes Built the Fox News Fear Factory*; Rolling Stone Magazine: May 2011[3]

Danny Duncan Collum. *Rising Common Ground Overcoming America's Color Lines; Just Faith, Inc. First Edition*: Jan 2006[4]

ABOUT THE AUTHOR

Justin Kase has periodically written articles over the last few years dealing with politics and current events. Outside of freelance writing he enjoys spending time with his wife and young daughter in his home state of Louisiana, where they reside.

www.ingramcontent.com/pod-product-compliance
Lightning Source LLC
Chambersburg PA
CBHW030427290526
45786CB00001B/178